A Pinch of Memory, A Dash of Love

Recipes from the Heart

Don McElwain

Good Health and Bon Appetit.

Don McElwain

BRUNDAGE PUBLISHING

A Pinch of Memory, A Dash of Love

Recipes from the Heart

Don McElwain

First Edition
Copyright © 2005 by Don McElwain

Copyright in the United States of America under all International and Pan-American Copyright Conventions.

All rights reserved. No part of this publication may be reproduced or utilized in any form or by any means, electronic, mechanical, photocopying, recording, or by any informational storage and retrieval system, without the written permission of the Publisher or Author, except for a reviewer who may quote brief passages in a review.

BRUNDAGE PUBLISHING
Room 203 Executive Office Building
33 West State Street
Binghamton, NY 13901
www.brundagepublishing.com

Edited by Patricia Bourdon
Cover Photography by Reed Roberts
Cover Design and Clip Art by Amanda Nord

Front cover recipe: "Coconut Cream Pie" page 3. Back cover recipes (left to right): "Ohio Buckeyes" page 112, "Lenora's Christmas Cookies" page 121, "Three-Cheese Spread" page 40, "Melba Toast" page 40, "Grand Marnier Sweet Potatoes" page 72, "Apricot Glazed Pork Tenderloin" page 70.

The "Men Making Meals" program was created by Judy Whiteman, Project Director for Caregiver Services, Broome County Office for the Aging and Michele Constable, Nutrition Educator, Cornell University Cooperative Extension of Broome County.

Coming Soon: The "Men Making Meals" course manual and program book, published by Brundage Publishing and written by Michele Constable; Judy Whiteman; and Ellen DeFay, Team Nutrition Coordinator. For more information contact Brundage Publishing.

Library of Congress Control Number: 2005921588

ISBN Number: 1-892451-36-0

Printed in the United States of America

In Loving Memory of an Irreplaceable Chef

This book is dedicated to the memory of my wife, Dittie Jo McElwain. Before we got married she warned me she barely knew how to boil water, but she had vastly underrated her abilities. She copied some of her Mother's recipes, bought a few books, and plunged ahead. She would constantly try new recipes, keeping those we liked, discarding those we did not, and occasionally adding some modifications of her own. I feel extremely blessed that I remained in her keeper file for almost fifty-two years, and somehow I feel I am still there.

I would like to quote from the last Hallmark card Dittie gave me on my seventy-fifth birthday:

"Love is forever between two hearts that share it…
as eternal as the tide that breaks upon the shore."

It is my sincere wish that the user of this book has found, or will find the kind of "forever love" Dittie and I knew.

Acknowledgements

In addition to those who contributed recipes, I would like to thank the people who have helped make this book possible, as no book of this type can be produced by one person alone:

None of this would have happened if Joanne had not sent me that notice from the newspaper about the class for senior men called "Men Making Meals." Perhaps she felt I would be relying on her to provide me with casseroles and such since I would now be doing my own cooking. Whatever the reason, I want to thank Joanne Wilczynski for propping me up and helping me to stand on my own two feet. This was the first step.

The next step was provided by Michele Constable who taught the class. I found her constant attitude of "of course you can" to be contagious. I finally began to believe it myself.

Kelly Greene, a reporter for the **Wall Street Journal**, attended one of our classes and prepared an article about the "Men Making Meals" program. The story appeared on the front page of that prestigious publication. That story was picked up by Laura Treciokas of the **NBC News**, and she and a crew from the **Today Show** came to interview Michele with a subsequent class and also me as a graduate of the course. Like a rolling snowball that keeps growing, Valerie Zehl of the Binghamton **Press & Sun-Bulletin** also published an interview with me.

The dominoes continued to fall when I received a call from Frank Resseguie, owner of Brundage Publishing, who persuaded me to attempt this book. I was more than ably assisted and encouraged by the staff at Brundage, particularly by Frank, who kept encouraging me, by Patricia Bourdon, who exercised great patience in providing the much needed editing, and by Amanda Nord, who provided the layouts and illustrations.

I would also like to extend thanks to many unnamed friends and family who encouraged and cajoled me when I was tempted to give up. Lastly, my thanks goes to the one who amassed all these recipes; my wife, **Dittie Jo McElwain**. I can only hope she would not have been embarrassed by the results of our combined efforts.

Recipes from the Heart

Re-introduced to Living ◇ by Don McElwain	i
"Men Making Meals" ◇ by Michele Constable	iii
Recipe Acknowledgments ◇ Family and Friends	v
Index ◇ Family Recipes	vii
Aroma of Innocence ◇ Cream and Custard Pies	1
Taste of Love ◇ Cafeteria Cooking	13
Savory Sneak Previews ◇ Canapés and Appetizers	23
Dessert Dilemma ◇ Desserts	41
Snowstorm Soups ◇ Warm-up Dishes	57
Our First Thanksgiving ◇ Special Dinners	67
Memorable Meals ◇ Breakfast Dishes	83
A Nibble of Prayer ◇ Casseroles	91
Bitten by the Sea ◇ Seafood	101
Ceremonial Flavor ◇ Holiday Treats	109
Peace, Love, and Beauty ◇ A Living Memory	125
Recipes that are Special to You ◇ My Special Recipes	127

RE-INTRODUCED TO LIVING
Don McElwain

In March 2003, I lost my wife to pneumonia while we were on vacation in Hawaii. We had been married for fifty-one years and eight months. As you may know from experience, or can imagine from experiences of others you know, such a catastrophe signals the end of one life and the beginning of a new life you must make for yourself. Family and friends can carry you for a while, but eventually you must continue with your new life and count on family and friends to be just that—family and friends.

In June, a friend sent me a newspaper clipping announcing a cooking class for senior men sponsored by the **Cornell University Cooperative Extension** and the Broome County **Office for the Aging**. She must have known the casseroles left in the freezer from before our trip, and those I had received from friends after, were almost gone. I took a chance that I was not too old to learn and signed up. Our teacher, Michele Constable, showed the class how to read and follow recipes. She taught us to check and see if we had all the necessary ingredients and how to prepare foods for cooking. We learned the art of folding, mixing, beating, slicing, chopping, mincing, and much, much more. These are basic things every homemaker knows and takes for granted. This was not my case, as I had never gotten beyond the cooking concept of "weenies and beanies."

Beyond the basics of cooking, however, she made us aware of the value of planning balanced meals including fruits, vegetables, meat, potatoes, and dessert. We also discussed which foods have which vitamins and minerals. These are things my wife, Dittie, used to do and I took for granted. More importantly, Michele taught me not to be afraid of going into the kitchen and planning for myself. Once I grasped this simple concept, I realized this idea could be applied to many other endeavors in my new life.

I had often helped Dittie with her routine housecleaning chores, but I only vacuumed the carpets while she dusted and cleaned the decorative pieces throughout our house. I knew she cleaned and polished the sterling silver every so often, but I had done no more than polish a few pieces to "help." There were houseplants to tend and flower beds to care for. How often did the carpets need cleaning? All of these and countless other little chores and nagging questions led me to the two big questions I needed to ask myself:

   1) Could I learn to perform all the tasks that needed to be done in order to maintain our home?

   2) Was remaining in the home Dittie and I had made together worth the effort?

The second question was easily answered. I loved the home we had shared for forty years and I did not want to give it up. Staying here was worth the effort. In answer to the first question, the realization I could learn to cook allowed me to believe I could learn the other aspects of living I would need to maintain our home. For example, I knew how to use the washer and dryer without overloading them, but I still had to learn how to iron clothes that are not "wash and wear." I still have not learned how to operate the sewing machine, but it is on my list of things to do. Only a few of the houseplants have died from my tending. I have learned to start new seedlings from old plants, and I have even transplanted some without killing them. Since I had "helped" Dittie with her weekly chores, I knew what to do, and it was easy to learn how to do them. It just takes me longer to do some things than it took her, and I had to learn to pattern my new life to do them on schedule.

About nine months after Dittie passed away, I hosted the three-table bridge group to which we had belonged. It was near Christmas and I had put up some holiday decorations, but not quite as many as usual. I got out Dittie's cookbook and prepared hors d'oeuvres and dessert. In trying to prove myself able to do this, I apparently got overanxious because I made twice the amount of canapés than I actually needed. I found myself still eating them for lunch, as well as for appetizers, a week after the party. I was informed later by two of the ladies in the bridge group that the first time you host it is normal for one to fix far more than is needed. They had done the same thing themselves. I am slowly learning I can adapt to my new life, but I realize I cannot do it all at once. Learning to have patience is sometimes as valuable as learning the task.

The important question that now remains is, can I continue to do all the tasks Dittie and I had previously divided between us? I intend to keep trying for a long time.

At one of my cooking classes Kelly Greene, a young reporter from the **Wall Street Journal**, came to meet us. She must have realized my ineptitude in the kitchen, because after she wrote her article she sent me a note saying, "As I reviewed my notes it became clear that you were getting more out of the class than anyone else there." Although that was probably because I had the least experience, I was flattered that my picture would accompany her article. I thanked her for providing me with my five minutes of fame.

Imagine my surprise when I received a call from Laura Treciokas of NBC's **Today Show** saying she would be following up on the **Wall Street Journal** article with a visit to one of Michele's classes. She also requested an interview at my house and asked if I could demonstrate some cooking skills I had learned. During the interview I baked a custard meringue pie for them from a recipe I found in *Taste of Home* magazine to which Dittie had subscribed. The pie smelled good in my kitchen and looked even better on the show, but they had to leave before it was cool enough to eat. Actually, it turned out pretty well. I then baked another one for the friend who had sent me the notice for the cooking class so long before.

My final bit of publicity came when Valerie Zehl of the Binghamton **Press & Sun-Bulletin** called requesting another interview. That interview appeared in the local newspaper on Thanksgiving Day. Thus, I have received a small degree of fame as a result of that clipping I received from a friend last June, but my real reward was learning I can survive in my new life. I know if I can be successful in overcoming my fears, others can do it too. For this I give thanks to Michele for giving me the courage to try. Thank you, Michele.

Over the past several years Dittie had collected many of the recipes she used, and saved them on our computer. It was an ongoing activity, which would probably never be completed. She then printed these out and collected them in a loose-leaf cookbook for her own use. These are the recipes that I began to use when I was forced to fend for myself. Although I still get many dinner invitations from friends, which provides me relief from my kitchen errors, I am beginning to reap the benefits of her efforts.

On the following pages I have related to you some memorable experiences of our life together and woven them in among Dittie's collection of recipes—recipes I offer you with "a pinch of memory and a dash of love."

Don McElwain

"MEN MAKING MEALS"
Michele Constable – Program Educator, Nutrition
Cornell University Cooperative Extension

When I was approached with the project of developing a series of lessons to teach basic cooking skills to senior men, I was intrigued by the idea. Many men over the age of sixty have never learned the cooking skills necessary to take care of themselves. They were not taught by their mothers because many household jobs were once separated by gender. After marriage, the men went on with their careers while their wives stayed home and established their domains in the kitchen. When men of this generation were faced with a wife who became ill or when they were widowed, suddenly eating—one of the basic necessities of life—became a daunting task, making a life already challenged by changed circumstances more difficult and less secure.

Planning the lessons for the course was not difficult. There are many different approaches to cooking, and even beginners come with some level of knowledge and practical experience. It seemed obvious the classes should include experiences and cooking techniques for different categories of foods: eggs, chicken, ground meat, fish, vegetables, soups, rice, and pasta. Desserts would be necessary as well—baking is a useful skill and a good opportunity to teach measuring. The men would need lessons on following recipes, chopping, mixing, and keeping foods safe from contamination. I wanted to include some nutritional information as well, especially as it relates to seniors, but primarily I wanted them to be able to plan meals from a number of simple main dishes.

I have been teaching these lessons to groups of men for three years. The lessons change a bit, the men change from class to class, and the dynamics of each group are different to some extent. The response, however, has always been very positive. Many of the men are retired professionals: doctors, lawyers, engineers, and teachers. Every one has been a gentleman. They have had successful careers and are capable, competent, and intelligent people. While I have certainly taught them some facts and skills, what many have expressed is the confidence they have learned in the previously foreign domain of the kitchen. They have learned there are many ways to adjust and attain good results in cooking. Further, and perhaps almost equally as important, the men have bonded socially and shared their stories with each other. Many stories relate to serving in the military and Kitchen Police duty. Then the stories get more personal, such as surviving the loss of a wife. As the classes continue, many wives are sending their husbands to learn a skill they may need in the future, and other men are coming on recommendation from friends and neighbors. For whatever reason, they are there together and they form bonds, share stories, and are open to new friendships.

I believe the men gain a lot from the classes. They learn to cook and by more than one method. They feel confident enough to try new recipes out at home, and they report back to me on what they have made. Nevertheless, I have gained more. I feel privileged to hear the men's stories and see the grace with which they face the difficulties that come with growing older. Their lives have touched mine, and I have become a better person because of the program.

RECIPE ACKNOWLEDGMENTS

Mom Mayer ◊ Wild Rice, Broccoli Puffs, Honey Glazed Carrots, Apricot Salad, Brunch for the Bunch, Lobster Dip, Braunschweiger Ball, Three-Cheese Spread, Shrimp Dip, Pineapple Cookies, Pie Crust, Ohio Buckeyes, Butterscotch Brownies ◊ **Mom Mac** ◊ Cherry Pudding, Strawberry Pie, Peanut Butter Swirls, Upside-down Raisin Pudding ◊ **Grandma Tucker** ◊ Seven Layer Cookies, Cream Pie, Custard Pie ◊ **Joyce Clark** ◊ Cream Cheese Tarts ◊ **Molly Jo Clark** ◊ Pumpkin Pie with Apricot, Coffee Walnut Toffee, Orange Rum Poached Pineapple with Yogurt, Spanish Custard, Lemon Bars, Shrimp Creole, Romoulade Sauce, Redfish Supreme, Tuna Lasagna, Grand Marnier Sweet Potatoes ◊ **Ryan Clark** ◊ Clay Pot Chicken, Cool Salsa, Italian Spinach, Great Lamb Rub, Rice Pilaf, Ultimate Meat Sauce, Ryan's Beef Brisket, Crispier Fries, Great Garlic Bread ◊ **Ben Clark** ◊ Guacamole ◊ **Andy** ◊ Taco Casserole ◊ **Billie Miller** ◊ Caramel Corn ◊ **Bobbie Furth** ◊ Panic ◊ **Hazel Flannigan** ◊ Strawberry Meringue Pie, Lemon Meringue Dessert, Cheese Olive Puffs ◊ **Doris Hayes** ◊ Vanilla Cream Mold with Caramel ◊ **Dot Jackson** ◊ Apple Cheese Pie ◊ **Ginny** ◊ Blitz Torte ◊ **Jan Bucklad** ◊ Cheese Potatoes, Homemade Toffee Candy, Championship Chocolate Chip Bars, Pepperoni Bread ◊ **Hanne Parsons** ◊ Butterscotch Pecan Squares ◊ **Helen Halbert** ◊ Ham & Broccoli Casserole ◊ **Jean Oltmanns** ◊ Honey Chicken Wings, Camembert Canapés, Blue Cheese Dip or Dressing, Blue Cheese Walnut Bites, Lemonade-Limeade Pie, Peanut Butter Pie, Coq au Vîn ◊ **Joy Snyder** ◊ Cheese Cake ◊ **Edie Strines** ◊ Hearty Turkey Vegetable Soup, Egg Casserole ◊ **Marcy Howe** ◊ Ruben Casserole ◊ **Marge Newton** ◊ Southern Pralines ◊ **Dolores Hansen** ◊ Grasshopper Cream, Frozen Cranberry Salad, Hot Tuna Casserole, Braunschweiger Ball #2, Coconut Torte ◊ **Marlene Fry** ◊ Apricot Fingers ◊ **Maryann Smith** ◊ Mexican Wedding Cakes ◊ **Babe Farbanish** ◊ Custard Cherry Pie, Food for the Angels ◊ **Miriam Biles** ◊ Gourmet Casserole ◊ **Shirley Schwartz** ◊ Dutch's Coffee Cake ◊ **Sue Carpenter** ◊ Chicken Breast ◊ **Mickey Ward** ◊ Chocolate Truffle Pie, Apple Coffee Cake, Macadamia Fudge Torte ◊ **Vicki Otto** ◊ Cocoons ◊ **Vivian Bou-Mourad** ◊ Pumpkin Pie Coffee Cake ◊ **Sandy Dimeo** ◊ Cheese Ball ◊ **Eileen O'Neil** ◊ Chocolate Trifle, Hot Asparagus Canapés ◊ **Bob Hansen** ◊ Scallops Seviche ◊ **Maggie Stankel** ◊ Stuffed Cherry Tomatoes ◊ **Jane Dillingham** ◊ Dried Beef Appetizer Pie ◊ **Corky** ◊ Hot & Good!, Cocktail Spread, Almond Fingers, Grand Marnier Dip ◊ **Marge Turna** ◊ Piña Colada Dip ◊ **Sara Wilson** ◊ Cheesy Crab Dip

Recipes Contributed by Cornell University Cooperative Extension

Pasta with Red Peppers, Greens, & Beans ◊ Italian Chicken Soup ◊ Italian Style Couscous ◊ Lentil Soup ◊ Macaroni & Cheese ◊ Mediterranean Eggplant Soup ◊ Mexican Corn & Tortilla Soup ◊ Mulligatawny Soup ◊ Mushroom Barley Soup ◊ New England Clam Chowder ◊ Pasta E Fagioli ◊ Pasta Primavera ◊ Pasta Salad ◊ Quick & Easy Homemade Spaghetti Sauce ◊ Spaghetti with Zucchini & Mozzarella ◊ Spicy Red Lentil Soup ◊ Three-Cheese Baked Ziti

CREAM AND CUSTARD PIES

Black Raspberry Silk Pie, 4
Cashew Pie, 5
Chocolate Amaretto Mousse, 5
Chocolate Mint Angel Pie, 5
Chocolate Mousse Pie, 6
Chocolate Truffle Pie, 6
Citrus Cheese Pie, 7
Coconut Cream Pie, 3
Cream Pie, 7
Custard Cherry Pie, 8
Custard Pie, 8
Easy Lemon Meringue, 8
Egg Nog Chiffon Pie, 8
Golden Dream Pie, 9
Lemonade-Limeade Pie, 9
Meringue Shell, 4
Peanut Butter Cream Pie, 9
Peanut Butter Pie, 10
Pie Crust, 4
Pumpkin Pie with Apricot, 10
Strawberry Pie, 11
Toffee-Bar Crunch Pie, 11
Totally Cookie Pie, 11

CAFETERIA COOKING

Beef Brisket, 16
Beef Stew, 16
Chicken Breast, 16
Fried Chicken, 17
Hot Chicken Salad, 17
Italian Dressing, 17
Italian Style Couscous, 17
Macaroni & Cheese, 18
Mom's Chicken, 18
Mozzarella Chicken, 18
One Dish Chicken & Rice Bake, 19
Parmesan Chicken Breast, 19
Pasta E Fagioli, 19
Pasta Primavera, 19
Pasta Salad, 20
Pasta with Red Peppers, Greens, & Beans, 20
Quick & Easy Spaghetti Sauce, 20
Spaghetti, Zucchini, & Mozzarella, 21
Three-Cheese Baked Ziti, 21

CANAPÉS AND APPETIZERS

Almond Fingers, 26
Angels in Blankets, 26
Artichoke Dip, 26
Artichokes & Mushrooms, 26
Artichoke Nibbles, 26
Blue Cheese Dip or Dressing, 27
Blue Cheese Log, 27
Blue Cheese Walnut Bites, 27
Braunschweiger Ball, 27
Braunschweiger Ball #2, 28
Brie en Croûte, 28
Burgundy Glazed Hots, 28
Camembert Canapé, 28
Caramelized Bacon, 28
Cheese & Bacon Puffs, 28
Cheese Ball, 29
Cheese Olive Puffs, 29
Cheese Snack Rounds, 29
Cheese Stuffed Mushrooms, 29
Cheesy Crab Dip, 29
Chestnuts with Bacon, 30
Chip Beef Fondue, 30
Cocktail Spread, 30
Crab Dip, 30
Crabmeat Canapés, 30
Crabmeat Sandwiches, 31
Crab Mousse, 31
Crab Stuffed Eggs, 31
Crispy Squares, 31
Cucumber Pecan Roll, 31
Cucumber Relish Boats, 32
Dilled Garden Dip, 32
Dill Dip, 32
Dried Beef Appetizer Pie, 32

Egg & Crab Mold, 32
Grand Marnier Dip, 33
Guacamole, 33
Ham & Cheese Appetizers, 33
Ham Balls, 33
Haute Garlic Bread, 34
Honey Chicken Wings, 34
Hot & Good!, 34
Hot Asparagus Canapés, 34
Hot Parmesan Snacks, 35
Impossible Quiche, 35
Italian Party Bites, 35
Layered Shrimp Dip, 35
Lobster Dip, 36
Marinated Mushrooms, 36
Melba Toast, 40
Mushroom Roll-Ups, 36
Marinated Cucumbers, 36
Pepperoni Bread, 36
Piña Colada Dip, 36
Pizza Quiche, 37

Rye Bread Dip, 37
Sausage Biscuit, 37
Sausage Rye Canapés, 37
Sausage Snack Wraps, 38
Scallops Seviche, 38
Sherry Potato Chip Dip, 38
Shrimp Dip, 38
Shrimp Spread, 38
Shrimp Toast, 39
Stuffed Cherry Tomatoes, 39
Stuffed Cukes, 39
Stuffed Mushrooms, 39
Swedish Meatballs, 39
Sweet & Sour Kielbasa, 39
Taco Dip, 40
Three-Cheese Ball, 40
Three-Cheese Spread, 40
Tomato-Mushroom Canapé, 40
Veggie Pizza, 40
Zucchini Hors D'oeuvres, 40

DESSERTS

Apple Bundt Cake, 44
Apple Cheese Pie, 44
Apricot Nut Bars, 44
Baked Peaches for Two, 45
Baked Pears with Marsala, 45
Blitz Torte, 45
Black Forest Torte, 46
Blueberry Torte, 46
Butterscotch Cheese Cake, 46
Caramel Peach Crunch, 47
Cheese Cake, 47
Cherry Pudding, 47
Chocolate Angel Pie, 47
Chocolate Crispy Ice Cream Pie, 48
Coconut Torte, 48
Cream Cheese Tarts, 48
Date Pudding, 48
Food for the Angels, 49
Frosty Mint Ice Cream Pie, 49
Frozen Grasshopper Pie, 49
Fruit Cocktail Dessert, 49
Girl Scout Refrigerator Cake, 50
Grasshopper Cream, 50

Lemon Bars, 50
Lemon Meringue Dessert, 50
Lemon Mousse, 51
Macadamia Fudge Torte, 51
Margarita Marinated
    Strawberries, 51
Miniature Cream Puffs, 52
New Napoleons, 52
Old Fashioned Lemon
    Pudding Cake, 52
Orange Rum Poached Pineapple with
    Yogurt, 53
Panic, 53
Peach Delight, 53
Peanut Butter Banana Crunch, 53
Pineapple Dessert, 54
Raspberry Delight, 54
Raspberry Ice Cream Pie, 54
Strawberry Dessert Nachos, 55
Strawberry Meringue Pie, 55
Upside-down Raisin Pudding, 55
Vanilla Cream Mold with
    Caramel Sauce, 56
Yum-Yum Dessert, 56

WARM-UP DISHES

Chili, 60
Cool Salsa, 60
Crispier Fries, 60
Great Garlic Bread, 61
Great Lamb Rub, 61
Hearty Turkey Vegetable Soup, 61
Italian Chicken Soup, 62
Italian Spinach, 62
Lentil Soup, 62

Mediterranean Eggplant Stew, 63
Mexican Corn & Tortilla Soup, 63
Mulligatawny Soup, 64
Mushroom Barley Soup, 64
New England Clam Chowder, 65
Rice Pilaf, 65
Spicy Red Lentil Soup, 65
Ultimate Meat Sauce, 65

SPECIAL DINNERS

Entrées

Apricot Glazed Pork Tenderloin, 70
Clay Pot Chicken, 70
Coq au Vîn, 70
Ryan's Beef Brisket, 71
Tiffin Style Beef Stroganoff, 71

Side Dishes

Broccoli Puffs, 71
Cheese Potatoes, 71
Crunchy Cheese Potatoes, 72
Glazed Pearl Onions, 72
Grand Marnier Sweet Potatoes, 72
Honey Glazed Carrots, 72
Oriental Cashew Asparagus, 73
Roasted Vidalia Onions, 73
Sweet Potatoes & Pecan Topping, 73
Wild Rice, 73

Salads

Apricot Salad, 74
Broccoli Salad, 74
Christmas Jell-O Salad, 74
Edie's Salad, 75
Frozen Bing-Cherry Salad, 75
Frozen Cranberry Salad, 75
Frozen Pineapple Salad, 75
Layered Orange Treat, 76
Oriental Salad, 76
24 Hour Salad, 76

Desserts

Banana Flambé au Grand Marnier, 77
Black Forest Cherry Cake, 77
Black Forest Crepes, 78
Chocolate Mint Dessert, 78
Chocolate Torte Royale, 79
Chocolate Trifle, 79
Heavenly Meringue Cake, 80
Mandarin Meringues, 80
Mousse au Kirsch, 81
Oriental Crackling Fruit, 81
Spanish Custard, 81
Strawberry Lemon Meringue Nests, 82

BREAKFAST DISHES

Apple Coffee Cake, 88
Brunch for the Bunch, 88
Dutch's Coffee Cake, 88
Egg Casserole, 89
French Toast, 89

Jewish Coffee Cake, 89
Morning Coffee Cake, 89
Mush, 90
Pumpkin Pie Coffee Cake, 90
Sausage & Egg Casserole, 90

CASSEROLES

Baked Sicilian Style Ziti, 94
Cheesy Taco Bake, 94
Chicken & Dressing, 94
Chicken Casserole, 94
Chipped Beef Casserole, 95
Chicken Broccoli Casserole, 95
Country Club Chipped Beef, 95
Crab & Shrimp Casserole, 95
Crabmeat Mousse, 96
Gourmet Casserole, 96

Green Rice Casserole, 96
Ham & Broccoli Casserole, 96
Heavenly Onion Casserole, 97
Hot Tuna Casserole, 97
Holupki Casserole, 97
Quiche Lorraine, 98
Ruben Casserole, 98
Taco Casserole, 98
Tuna Chow Mein, 99
Turkey Casserole, 99

SEAFOOD

Crabmeat in Shells, 104
Crab Nichola, 104
Crab Stuffed Mushrooms, 104
Fish Marinade, 104
Grilled Salmon with Lime
    Butter, 105
Redfish Supreme, 105

Romoulade Sauce, 105
Salmon with Lemon Chive
    Sauce, 106
Scallops, Asparagus, & Mushrooms, 106
Shrimp Creole, 106
Seafood Chowder, 107
Tuna Lasagna, 107

HOLIDAY TREATS

Candies

Almond Rolls, 113
Apricot Fingers, 113
Caramel Candy, 113
Caramel Corn, 113
Chocolate Peanut Butter Cups, 114
Coffee Walnut Toffee, 114
Fudgie Scotch Ring, 114
Homemade Toffee Candy, 115
Mom's Fudge, 115
Nut Brittle, 115
Ohio Buckeyes, 112
Peanut Butter Peanut Brittle, 115
Sea Foam, 116
Southern Pralines, 116
Turtles, 116

Cookies

Bourbon Balls, 117
Brown Sugar Crisps, 117

Butterscotch Brownies, 117
Butterscotch Pecan Squares, 117
Championship Chocolate
    Chip Bars, 118
Chocolate Chip Crisps, 118
Chocolate Chip, Oatmeal, & Peanut
    Butter Cookies, 118
Coconut Thumbprints, 119
Cocoons, 119
Congo Cookies, 119
Cream Cheese Cookies, 120
Double Crunchers, 120
Fudgie Peanut Butter Bars, 120
Lenora's Christmas Cookies, 121
Merry Cheese Bars, 121
Mexican Wedding Cakes, 121
Pineapple Cookies, 121
Peanut Butter Swirls, 122
Pecan Crispies, 122
Pecan Turtle Cookies, 122
Seven Layer Cookies, 122
Sour Cream Cookies, 123
Viennese Walnut Cookies, 123

Cream and Custard Pies

AROMA OF INNOCENCE

Childhood Memory ◊ The Barbeque

One of my favorite childhood memories is the wonderful aroma of ham and pork being barbequed on the spit in front of a grate holding a bed of coals at my grandparents' restaurant. With this arrangement, a pan could be placed under the meat and basting sauce as they were being barbequed to catch any drippings. Thus, there was no smoke or flare-up to spoil the aroma or flavor.

The restaurant was called Vertner's Barbecue and was located on the Dixie Highway in Beaverdam, Ohio. We lived in the rear of the restaurant, and I have fond memories of waking up in the morning to the aroma of pies baking in the oven, which was in my bedroom.

The menu was quite limited. Lunch was the "Blue Plate Special," which consisted of barbequed ham or pork, potato salad, and bread and butter, and cost twenty-five cents. The dinner menu was the same with an option of fried steak or a pork chop in place of the barbequed meat. This cost fifty cents. A cup of coffee was five cents extra, and for another ten cents you could get a piece of pie. A piece was one fourth of a 9-inch pie.

Even during the Great Depression, people would travel as far as thirty or forty miles to eat at Vertner's Barbecue. The lunches and dinners were popular, but many people came for a piece of Grandma Vertner's homemade Coconut Cream Pie. I do not have her recipe for that pie, mostly described as a bit of this and a bit of that, but Dittie's Grandma Tucker's recipe is very similar to Grandma Vertner's, as I recall:

COCONUT CREAM PIE

9-inch pie crust
(recipe page 4)
⅓ cup flour
⅔ cup sugar
¼ teaspoon salt

2 cups milk
2 tablespoons butter
3 lightly beaten egg yolks
½ teaspoon vanilla extract
½ cup shredded coconut

Preheat oven to 450 degrees F. Place pie crust in un-greased pie pan and press firmly against bottom and sides of pan. Trim excess crust and flute edges. Bake for 8 to 10 minutes, or til lightly browned. Mix the dry ingredients in the top of a double boiler.

Reduce oven to 350 degrees F. Bring milk to a scald (about 175 to 180 degrees F on thermometer). Gradually add milk to dry ingredients, stirring constantly til thick. Add butter and egg yolks. Cook for 2 minutes. Add vanilla extract. Pour mixture into cooled pre-baked crust.

Top filling with meringue made by beating egg whites til stiff, but not dry. Sprinkle coconut over meringue.

Bake for about 10 minutes, or til meringue is slightly brown. Served 4 at the barbecue. Serves 6 today.

Pie Crust

Note: Prepared pie crusts are available in most grocery stores, and that is what I generally use. If you want to try your hand, however, you might use the following recipe.

Double Crust

2 cups flour
1 teaspoon salt
⅔ cup shortening
6 to 8 tablespoons cold water

Single Crust

1 to 1 ½ cups flour
½ teaspoon salt
½ cup shortening
4 to 6 tablespoons cold water

Mix ingredients in medium bowl, using your hands to knead the dough, or simply pulse with a food processor. Do not knead any longer than necessary to combine the ingredients or the dough will be tough instead of light and flaky.

Lightly flour your board or countertop and roll out each crust (one for a single crust and two for a double crust) with a rolling pin to approximately 11 to 12 inches in diameter for a 9-inch pie pan.

If you don't have a rolling pin, a wine bottle has been known to be used.

Meringue Shell

(This is sometimes used as a pie shell.)

3 egg whites
¼ teaspoon cream of tartar
½ cup sugar

Preheat oven to 225 degrees F. In a small bowl beat egg whites and cream of tartar on high speed til soft peaks form.

Sprinkle in sugar, 2 tablespoons at a time, beating well after each addition til sugar dissolves. Beat til whites stand in stiff, glossy peaks. Spoon meringue into pie pan, maintaining the meringue to the approximate shape of the pan.

Bake meringue for 2 ½ hours. Turn off oven and let meringue remain in oven for 1 hour to dry. Remove and allow meringue to cool on a wire rack.

If not being used right away, the meringue may be stored at room temperature in an airtight container.

Black Raspberry Silk Pie

9-inch pie shell, baked
2 cups black raspberries
3 eggs, beaten slightly
1 ½ cups whipping cream
¾ cup sugar
1 teaspoon vanilla extract
Pinch of salt

Preheat oven to 425 degrees F. Combine eggs, whipping cream, sugar, vanilla extract, and salt. Purée raspberries in blender and strain. Add berries to mixture. Make sure mixture is not too frothy.

Pour into a pre-baked 9-inch pie shell. Bake 10 minutes at 425 degrees F, then 35 minutes at 325 degrees F. Serves 10.

CASHEW PIE

9-inch unbaked pie crust
¾ cup packed brown sugar
2 tablespoons butter, softened
¾ cup corn syrup
1 teaspoon vanilla extract
3 eggs
1 cup chopped cashews

Heat oven to 350 degrees F. In large bowl beat brown sugar and butter at high speed til light and fluffy.

Add corn syrup and vanilla extract. Beat at medium speed til smooth. Beat in eggs one at a time, blending well after each egg. Stir in nuts.

Pour into pie shell. Bake for 45 to 50 minutes, or til top of pie is deep golden brown. Serves 6.

CHOCOLATE AMARETTO MOUSSE PIE

12 ounces semisweet chocolate chips
¼ cup butter
14 ounces sweetened condensed milk
¼ teaspoon salt
¼ cup water
¼ cup amaretto liqueur
2 cups heavy cream
Sliced almonds for garnish

Line a 9-inch pie pan with aluminum foil. Press the foil firmly against the surface of the pan, making the foil as smooth as possible.

Melt 1 cup of the chocolate pieces with 2 tablespoons of butter in small pan over very low heat. Pour into foil-lined plate and quickly smooth over the bottom and up the sides. Place in the freezer til firm, about 30 minutes.

Meanwhile prepare filling. Combine remaining chocolate and butter with sweetened condensed milk and salt in medium saucepan. Cook stirring constantly over low heat til chocolate is melted. Stir in water gradually.

Cook stirring constantly over medium heat for 5 minutes. Add amaretto, cook and stir for 5 more minutes, or til thickened. Cool to room temperature. To hasten cooling, place pan over ice and water and stir occasionally for 10 minutes. Beat cream in medium bowl til stiff. Remove and refrigerate ½ cup for garnish.

Stir half of the remaining whipped cream briskly into chocolate mixture to loosen slightly and fold in the other half. When chocolate shell is firm, lift gently from pan with foil. Carefully peel off the foil and place shell on serving plate.

Spoon the filling into the shell and garnish with the sliced almonds and reserved whipped cream. Chill til set, about 3 to 3 ½ hours. Serves 6.

CHOCOLATE MINT ANGEL PIE

¾ cup chocolate chips
¾ cup grasshopper mix
1 cup heavy cream, whipped

Make a meringue shell and then sprinkle ½ cup pecans on top.

Melt chocolate in small saucepan over low heat. Stir in grasshopper mix and cook til slightly thick. Cool.

Fold in whipped cream and pour into shell. Chill 2 to 3 hours or overnight. Serves 6.

Chocolate Mousse Pie

This is a little complicated, but quite good!

Crust

3 cups chocolate wafer crumbs
½ cup unsalted butter, melted

Filling

1 pound semisweet chocolate
2 eggs
4 egg yolks
2 cups whipping cream
6 tablespoons powdered sugar
4 egg whites

Chocolate Leaves

8 ounces semisweet chocolate
1 tablespoon vegetable oil
Waxy leaves, such as Camellia
2 cups whipping cream
Additional sugar

Crust

Combine crumbs and butter and press into bottom and completely up sides of 10-inch spring form pan. Refrigerate 30 minutes or chill in freezer.

Filling

Soften chocolate in top of double boiler over simmering water. Let cool til lukewarm (95 degrees F). Add whole eggs and mix well. Add yolks and mix til thoroughly blended.

Whip cream with powdered sugar til soft peaks form. Beat egg whites til stiff but not dry. Stir just a little of the cream and egg whites into chocolate mixture to lighten.

Fold in remaining cream and whites til completely incorporated. Turn into crust and chill at least 6 hours, or preferably overnight.

Chocolate Leaves

Melt chocolate and shortening in top of double boiler. Using spoon, generously coat underside of leaves. Chill or freeze til firm.

Whip remaining 2 cups whipping cream with sugar til quite stiff. Loosen crust on all sides and remove spring form. Spread all but ½ cup whipped cream over top of mousse. Pipe rosettes in center with rest of whipped cream.

Separate chocolate from leaves, starting at stem of leaf. Place around on top. Cut pie into wedges. Serves 8 to 10.

Chocolate Truffle Pie

½ cup pecan pieces, toasted and coarsely chopped
8-inch chocolate crumb crust

Caramel Layer

¾ cup (5 ounces) unwrapped caramels
¼ cup evaporated milk

Truffle Layer

1 ½ cups (9 ounces) chocolate chips
1 cup heavy cream
3 tablespoons butter
Whipped cream for garnish

Sprinkle pecans on crust. In small saucepan heat caramels with evaporated milk til melted and mixture is smooth. Pour over pecans.

In medium saucepan heat chocolate chips, cream, and butter til melted and mixture is smooth. Pour over caramel layer. Refrigerate 4 hours. Serves 10.

Citrus Cheese Pie

9-inch pie crust
1 lemon pudding mix
4 tablespoons melted butter
4 ounces cream cheese, whipped
2 tablespoons sugar
1 teaspoon shredded orange peel
½ teaspoon vanilla extract
3 ounces orange gelatin
Whipped topping
1 orange, peeled and sectioned

Bake pie shell and cool. Prepare lemon pudding mix according to package directions for pie filling; except use 1 whole egg, slightly beaten, in place of the 2 egg yolks called for, and omit meringue. Stir butter into hot pie filling, cover, and cool to room temperature.

Blend whipped cream cheese with sugar, orange peel, and vanilla extract. Spread evenly in bottom of pie shell. Prepare orange gelatin according to directions and cool til mixture begins to set.

Beat lemon pie filling til smooth. Spread evenly over cream cheese layer. Top with 1 cup orange gelatin (save the rest for a salad).

Chill pie thoroughly. Place whipped topping in center of pie and garnish with orange sections. Serves 6.

Cream Pie

9-inch pie crust
⅓ cup flour
⅔ cup sugar
¼ teaspoon salt
2 cups milk
2 tablespoons butter
3 lightly beaten egg yolks
½ teaspoon vanilla extract

Preheat oven to 450 degrees F. Place pie crust into un-greased pie pan (glass recommended). Press crust firmly against bottom and sides of pan. Trim excess crust and flute edges.

Bake for 8 to 10 minutes or til lightly browned. Allow to cool before filling.

Reduce oven to 350 degrees F. Mix the dry ingredients in the top of a double boiler. Bring milk to scald and gradually add to the dry ingredients, stirring constantly til thick. Add butter and egg yolks. Cook for 2 minutes. Add vanilla extract.

Pour mixture into pre-baked crust. Top filling with meringue made by beating egg whites til stiff, but not dry. Bake for about 10 minutes, or til meringue is slightly brown. Serves 6.

Cream Pie Variations

Butterscotch

Substitute 1 cup packed brown sugar for granulated sugar.

Chocolate

Increase sugar to 1 cup and add 2 squares of unsweetened chocolate to scalded milk til melted.

Banana

Slice 2 to 3 bananas and add to cream filling.

Coconut Variation

Add 1 cup shredded coconut to filling and sprinkle ½ cup over meringue before browning.

Caramel

Caramelize ¼ cup sugar til golden in color and smooth. Add scalded milk gradually and stir til thoroughly blended.

Custard Cherry Pie

9-inch pie crust
1 cup cherry pie filling
2 eggs, beaten
½ cup sugar
¼ cup melted butter
2 teaspoons lemon juice
¼ teaspoon vanilla extract
½ cup flaked coconut

Preheat oven to 375 degrees F. Make single pie crust in 9-inch pan. Spoon cherry pie filling into unbaked crust. Bake for 30 minutes.

Combine remaining ingredients in large bowl and carefully pour over cherries. Return to oven and bake 20 to 25 minutes more. Serves 6.

Custard Pie

3 eggs
1 pint milk
½ cup sugar

Preheat oven to 350 degrees F. In large mixing bowl beat eggs til foamy. Add milk and beat hard. Add sugar and beat again. Pour into unbaked pie shell and sprinkle nutmeg on top. Bake for 45 minutes, or til firm. Serves 6.

Caramel Custard Variation

Use ½ cup packed brown sugar mixed with 1 tablespoon flour and place in bottom of shell under the custard.

Easy Lemon Meringue Pie

15 ounces sweetened condensed milk
2 eggs separated
2 tablespoons sugar
¼ teaspoon lemon extract or ½ cup lemon juice
Grated rind of 1 lemon

Preheat oven to 350 degrees F. In large bowl blend milk, juice, and egg yolks. Pour into baked 8-inch pie shell.

Cover with meringue made by beating egg whites til stiff, but not dry. Add sugar.

Bake for about 10 minutes or til brown. Chill. Serves 6.

Egg Nog Chiffon Pie

1 envelope unflavored gelatin mixed with ¼ cup cold water
½ cup sugar
½ teaspoon salt
1 ¼ cups milk
3 eggs, separated
1 tablespoon vanilla extract
½ cup heavy cream, whipped
¼ teaspoon cream of tartar
½ cup sugar
2 teaspoons rum flavoring
¼ teaspoon nutmeg

Mix ½ cup sugar, salt, and milk together in medium saucepan and cook over low heat, stirring constantly til scalded. Remove from heat and stir ½ of the mixture into 3 slightly beaten egg yolks. Blend in rest of mixture and cook over low heat, stirring til it boils. Remove from heat and stir in softened gelatin. Cool.

When mixture is partially set, beat with rotary beater til smooth. Blend in 1 tablespoon vanilla extract and ½ cup whipped cream. Pour into cooled pie shell.

Top pie with 3 egg whites beaten together with cream of tartar, ½ cup sugar, and rum flavoring. Sprinkle nutmeg on top. Serves 6.

GOLDEN DREAM PIE

3 eggs
¾ cup orange juice
1 envelope unflavored gelatin
⅓ cup sugar
Pinch of salt
2 tablespoons grated orange peel
¼ cup Galliano
¼ cup Cointreau
¼ teaspoon cream of tartar
¼ cup sugar
1 cup heavy cream, whipped
1 baked 9-inch graham cracker crust
½ cup toasted coconut

Separate egg whites while cool and let them warm to room temperature.

In small saucepan combine orange juice and gelatin. Stir to blend. Add ⅓ cup sugar, salt, and egg yolks. Stir to blend. Cook over low heat stirring constantly til gelatin is dissolved and mixture is hot, but not simmering. Do not boil. Remove from heat.

Add Galliano, Cointreau, and orange peel. Stir well. Refrigerate til mixture begins to thicken, about 1 hour.

Add cream of tartar and a pinch of salt to egg whites. Beat til soft peaks form. Sprinkle half of ¼ cup sugar over the egg whites. Beat til incorporated. Repeat with remaining sugar. Fold thickened gelatin mixture into egg whites. Fold half the whipped cream into gelatin mixture.

Pour into pie crust. Sprinkle toasted coconut around rim of pie. Refrigerate for several hours. Garnish with remaining whipped cream. Serves 8 to 10.

LEMONADE–LIMEADE PIE

1 can frozen lemonade-limeade
1 can sweetened condensed milk
8 ounces whipped topping

Mix the above together in large bowl and place in graham cracker crust. Chill 4 hours. Serves 6.

PEANUT BUTTER CREAM PIE

8 ounces cream cheese, softened
¾ cup powdered sugar
½ cup creamy peanut butter
6 tablespoons milk
8 ounces whipped topping
9-inch graham pie crust
¼ cup chopped peanuts

In large bowl beat cream cheese til fluffy. Add sugar and peanut butter. Mix well. Gradually add milk.

Fold in whipped topping and spoon into crust. Top with peanuts. Serves 6.

PEANUT BUTTER PIE

4 ounces cream cheese, softened
½ cup creamy peanut butter
⅓ cup powdered sugar
8 ounces whipped topping

Mix all ingredients in large bowl til smooth and pour into chocolate cookie pie crust. Chill or freeze.

Drizzle chocolate syrup over top before serving. Serves 6.

PUMPKIN PIE WITH APRICOT

Crust

1 ½ cups flour
½ cup powdered sugar
1 stick of chilled butter, cut into pieces
3 tablespoons whipping cream

Preheat to 350 degrees F. Blend the first 3 ingredients in a food processor til they resemble coarse meat.

Add whipping cream and process til moist clumps form. Gather into a ball and flatten into a disk. Wrap in plastic and chill 15 minutes.

Roll out dough on floured surface to a 14-inch round. Transfer to 9-inch pie pan and flute edges. Freeze 15 minutes.

Line crust with foil, pressing firmly. Bake til set, about 10 minutes. Remove foil.

Bake til pale brown, 10 minutes more. Reduce oven to 325 degrees F.

Filling

¾ cup sugar
1 tablespoon cornstarch
2 teaspoons cinnamon
¾ teaspoon ginger
¼ teaspoon salt
16 ounces solid packed pumpkin
¾ cup whipping cream
½ cup sour cream
3 large eggs, beaten

Use a whisk and mix first 5 ingredients in large bowl til no lumps remain. Blend in pumpkin, whipping cream, sour cream, and eggs.

Spread ¼ cup apricot preserves over crust. Pour in filling. Bake at 325 degrees F til filling puffs at edges and center is almost set, about 55 minutes.

Cool on rack, cover, and chill (can be made 1 day ahead). Serves 8 to 10.

STRAWBERRY PIE

1 cup water
1 cup sugar
2 tablespoons corn syrup
3 tablespoons cornstarch
2 tablespoons strawberry gelatin
Red food coloring
1 quart strawberries, cleaned with stems removed

Over medium heat cook the first 4 ingredients in a saucepan til thick. Add gelatin and food coloring, blend well. Remove from heat and allow time to cool.

Combine with strawberries and place in baked 9-inch pie shell. Chill and serve. Serves 6.

TOFFEE-BAR CRUNCH PIE

1 ½ cups half-and-half (or light cream or milk)
1 package vanilla instant pudding and pie filling
3 ½ cups whipped topping
1 cup chopped chocolate covered toffee bars
1 graham cracker crust

Pour half-and-half (or light cream or milk) into large bowl. Add vanilla instant pudding and pie filling.

Beat with wire whisk til well-blended, less than 1 minute. Let stand 5 minutes.

Fold in whipped topping and chopped toffee bars. Spoon into crust. Freeze til firm, about 6 hours or overnight.

Remove from freezer and let stand 10 minutes to soften before serving. Store in freezer. Serves 6.

TOTALLY COOKIE PIE

2 eggs
½ cup flour
½ cup sugar
½ cup packed brown sugar
1 cup butter, melted and cooled to room temperature
6 ounces chocolate chips
1 cup chopped walnuts
9-inch unbaked pie shell
Whipped topping

Preheat oven to 325 degrees F. In large bowl beat eggs til foamy. Beat in flour, sugar, and brown sugar til well-blended.

Blend in melted butter. Stir in chips and nuts and pour into pie shell.

Bake for 1 hour. Serve with whipped topping or ice cream.

Can be frozen. Serves 6.

Cafeteria Cooking

TASTE OF LOVE

How We Met ◇ The Cafeteria

When I entered The Ohio State University in 1946, there were thousands of other veterans eager to take advantage of the GI Bill. Existing facilities were not intended to handle such a large influx of new students. Proving, however, that every cloud has a silver lining, male students could now buy meal tickets at the girls' dormitories. Men were permitted only in the cafeteria, the adjoining recreation room, and the entrance lobby. Men were never permitted above the first floor; the house mother made sure of that.

The recreation room was a large room with the usual ping pong table, a well-used upright piano, a few scattered tables with chairs, and a small stage at one end with a 78 RPM record player. It seemed records were always being played. One day, I was on the stage talking to Joyce, who was playing the records, when I noticed a name written on adhesive tape stuck to the label of each record. The name was Dittie Jo Mayer. This unique name intrigued me so much that I told Joyce I would like to meet her. It turned out they were suitemates, and a meeting was easily arranged. Not long afterwards I asked Dittie to a dance, then to an occasional movie, and soon we were dating each other exclusively.

There were very few students who had cars in those days. As a result it was quite common to double or triple date with four or six people cozily squeezed into one car. On one such triple date I whispered to Dittie, "Will you marry me?" The other girl sitting in the back seat with us said, "What?" Neither of us answered her because Dittie had whispered "Yes." We were married in 1951 after I graduated. How fortunate for me that I noticed her name on the record label.

The college cafeteria prepared good, nourishing food in large quantities and for a reasonable price, in consideration of the budget limitations of the majority of the students. Many meals utilized chicken in various ways because it was relatively inexpensive and nourishing and could be prepared in many ways. Entrées with beef and pork were perhaps less numerous, but were generally available. Cafeteria serving, of course, also lacks the opportunity for the attractive presentation that can be provided with individual service. The recipes listed below represent some of the dishes you might see in a cafeteria plus, perhaps, some you might not.

BEEF BRISKET

2 to 3 pounds brisket of beef (first cut)
1 to 2 teaspoons Worcestershire sauce
Seasoned salt to taste
Small foil hot bag
1 to 2 tablespoons flour
1 to 2 cups beef broth, not condensed

Preheat oven to 250 degrees F. Place 1 to 2 tablespoons of flour in bag and flip bag over to distribute the flour a bit. This keeps the meat from sticking to the bag. Place bag on a cookie sheet (for support). Trim fat off brisket. Sprinkle with Worcestershire sauce and seasoned salt.

Place seasoned brisket in the foil bag. Seal the bag well.

Bake for 5 to 8 hours. Remove brisket from bag and let it rest on a cutting board.

For gravy pour drippings from bag into pot. Add broth and bring to a boil.

For thicker gravy whisk 1 tablespoon flour with about ¼ cup broth and add it slowly to the boiling broth and drippings (pour through fine mesh sieve, stirring constantly to remove lumps, if necessary).

To serve cut brisket across grain. Serve with gravy or heated barbeque sauce. Serves 4 to 8.

Leftovers make very tasty barbeque beef sandwiches.

BEEF STEW

3 carrots cut into bite-size pieces
3 potatoes cut into bite-size pieces
1 small onion, cut up
1 celery stick, cut in half
14-ounce can diced tomatoes
2 pounds stew beef, cut into 1 ½-inch chunks
2 cups beef broth
Spice (see below)

Put everything in a crock pot and cook on low for 10 to 12 hours or on high for 4 to 5 hours. Remove bay leaves, if used, and celery.

For a thicker consistency coat the meat in flour and brown in a couple of tablespoons of cooking oil before adding the rest of the ingredients. Serves 8 to 10.

Spice

1 teaspoon Worcestershire sauce
1 clove garlic
2 bay leaves, optional
Dash of allspice
½ teaspoon pepper
Salt to taste (depending on how salty the broth is)

You can also use a seasoning mix that comes in an envelope if you prefer.

CHICKEN BREAST

6 boneless chicken breast halves
½ cup chopped dried beef
6 slices bacon, cut in half
1 can condensed mushroom soup
½ cup sour cream

Preheat oven to 325 degrees F. Cover bottom of 13 x 9-inch casserole dish with chopped dried beef (blanch if you want). Place boned chicken breast on top of chopped beef and 2 half slices of bacon on top of each chicken breast.

Mix mushroom soup and sour cream and place on top. Bake for 3 hours. Serves 6.

Fried Chicken

Favorite cuts of chicken (legs, thighs, breasts)
Flour or corn meal, enough to coat chicken
Butter, margarine, or cooking oil to grease skillet

Lightly dredge chicken in flour or corn meal. Heat grease in a medium-hot skillet to ⅛-inch deep. Carefully add chicken pieces to the pan and sear on all sides. Reduce temperature to medium and cook covered or uncovered til done (20 to 30 minutes, depending on size of pieces). Remove chicken from pan.

Instead of flour or cornmeal the chicken may be dipped in beer batter. Mix ½ can of beer with 1 cup of flour. Follow above procedure for cooking.

Hot Chicken Salad

2 cups cubed chicken
2 cups celery cut in 1 ½-inch pieces
½ cup toasted slivered almonds
1 cup mayonnaise
1 cup potato chips, crushed
½ cup grated cheese for top
½ teaspoon salt
½ teaspoon accent
2 tablespoons grated onion
2 tablespoons lemon juice

Preheat oven to 325 degrees F. In large bowl mix all ingredients except cheese and potato chips. Pile mixture lightly in buttered 13 x 9-inch baking dish and sprinkle top with cheese and chips. Bake for 30 minutes. Do not over bake. Celery will be crunchy.

For best flavor do not use left-over chicken. Serves 6.

Italian Dressing

¼ cup vinegar
3 tablespoons vegetable oil
⅛ teaspoon garlic powder
⅛ teaspoon pepper
½ teaspoon oregano

Combine all ingredients in a container with lid and shake to blend thoroughly, or combine in a small bowl and mix well with a spoon. Cover and refrigerate. Makes ½ cup of dressing.

Italian Style Couscous

1 tablespoon olive oil
½ green pepper, chopped
½ cup onion, chopped
28-ounce can whole tomatoes; chopped, with juice
16-ounce can garbanzo beans, rinsed and drained
1 ½ teaspoons dried basil
½ teaspoon dried oregano
½ teaspoon garlic powder
¼ teaspoon black pepper
¼ teaspoon paprika
¼ cup grated Parmesan cheese
1 ½ cups couscous, uncooked
1 ½ cups boiling water

In a large saucepan or skillet, sauté onions and green peppers in olive oil til soft. Add tomatoes, garbanzo beans, basil, oregano, garlic powder, black pepper, and paprika. Heat to boiling, reduce heat, and simmer for 10 minutes. Meanwhile, place dry couscous in a heat proof bowl. Add boiling water and stir. Cover and let stand for 5 minutes. Remove cover and fluff with fork. Serve tomato and bean mixture over couscous. Sprinkle with cheese. Serves 4.

MACARONI & CHEESE

1 pound elbow macaroni, cooked
2 ½ cups skim milk
2 tablespoons margarine
2 tablespoon flour
2 ½ cups low-fat mozzarella cheese, grated
1 cup low-fat cottage cheese
½ cup cheddar cheese, shredded
¾ cup bread crumbs

Preheat oven to 375 degrees F. Boil macaroni according to package directions, drain, and set aside.

Combine grated cheeses in medium bowl. (Keep cottage cheese separate for now.)

Melt margarine in a medium saucepan over low heat. Blend in flour and then slowly add milk, stirring constantly over medium heat til sauce thickens.

Add grated cheeses to white sauce, except for ½ cup, and make cheese sauce by stirring til cheese is melted. Mix bread crumbs with ½ cup of the grated cheese in small bowl.

Combine macaroni and cheese sauce in large casserole dish. Top with grated cheese and bread crumb mixture.

Bake til top is golden brown, about 30 to 40 minutes.

MOM'S CHICKEN

6 chicken breasts, boned and skinned
1 can cream of chicken soup
½ cup white wine
6 slices American cheese
½ package stuffing mix (8 ounces)
¼ pound butter

Preheat oven to 350 degrees F. Place chicken in baking dish with slice of cheese on each breast. Mix wine and soup and pour over chicken. Sprinkle stuffing mix on top. Melt butter and drizzle over top. Bake 1 hour. Should be bubbly. Serves 6.

MOZZARELLA CHICKEN

4 chicken cutlets, pounded thin
1 pound mushrooms, sliced
1 sweet red pepper, diced
2 cloves garlic, crushed in press
4 thin slices mozzarella cheese
Salt and pepper to taste

Heat 1 tablespoon olive oil in large skillet. Sprinkle chicken on both sides with salt and pepper.

Add chicken to skillet and cook 4 to 5 minutes, turning halfway through. Remove chicken from skillet to plate and keep warm.

Add another tablespoon of oil to skillet and cook mushrooms and red pepper over medium-high heat til softened, about 5 minutes.

Stir in garlic, ½ teaspoon salt, and ⅛ teaspoon pepper. Cook 1 minute. Return chicken and any accumulated juices to skillet.

Place slice of cheese on top of each, cover, and cook over medium-low heat til cheese melts. To serve spoon mushroom mixture over chicken. Serves 4.

ONE DISH CHICKEN & RICE BAKE

1 can cream of mushroom soup
1 cup water
¾ cup uncooked regular rice
¼ teaspoon paprika
¼ teaspoon pepper
4 skinless, boneless chicken breast halves

In a 2-quart baking dish mix soup, water, rice, paprika, and pepper. Place chicken on rice mixture. Sprinkle with additional paprika and pepper. Cover and bake at 375 degrees F for 45 minutes, or til chicken and rice are done. Serves 4.

PARMESAN CHICKEN BREAST

6 boneless chicken breast halves
2 tablespoons margarine
½ cup Parmesan cheese
¼ cups dry bread crumbs
1 teaspoon oregano
1 teaspoon parsley flakes

Preheat oven to 400 degrees F. Grease 13 x 9-inch baking dish. Coat chicken first in melted margarine and then with dry ingredients. Place in baking dish and bake for 20 to 25 minutes. Serves 6.

PASTA E FAGIOLI

1 tablespoon olive oil
1 medium onion, chopped
28-ounce can diced tomatoes
½ teaspoon salt
⅛ teaspoon black pepper
1 teaspoon rosemary, crumbled
½ teaspoon sage
1 cup uncooked pasta; ditalini, elbows, or small shells
2 (15-ounce) cans cannelloni beans, drained and rinsed

Trito

½ cup Italian parsley, chopped
4 garlic cloves
½ cup carrot, chopped
2 tablespoons olive oil

Blend ingredients for trito in small bowl til smooth. Set aside. Sauté onion with olive oil in large skillet til transparent. Add trito and continue cooking til slightly brown. Add undrained tomatoes, beans, salt, pepper, and herbs. Simmer for 15 minutes. Meanwhile, cook pasta and then drain. Add pasta just before serving. Serves 5.

PASTA PRIMAVERA

1 tablespoon oil
1 cup chopped onions
2 cups cut up broccoli
1 cup sliced carrot
1 cup chopped celery
2 cups chopped tomato
¼ teaspoon salt
1 teaspoon dried basil
¼ teaspoon black pepper
½ teaspoon garlic powder
1 pound uncooked spaghetti
¼ cup Parmesan cheese

Fill large pot ⅔ full with water and bring to a boil. Cook spaghetti til tender and drain when done. In a medium skillet cook hard vegetables in oil for about 5 minutes.

Add medium vegetables and continue cooking for 3 to 4 more minutes. Add salt, pepper, garlic powder, and basil (and any soft vegetables). Continue cooking for 2 to 3 minutes. Combine cooked spaghetti with vegetables. Sprinkle Parmesan cheese on top. Serves 5.

Pasta Salad

8 ounces uncooked spiral pasta
1 celery stalk
1 small onion
½ green or red pepper
1 tomato
16-ounce can garbanzo beans, rinsed and drained
2 tablespoons Parmesan cheese
¼ cup low-fat, low-salt Italian dressing; or try Italian dressing recipe (page 17)

Fill a 2-quart saucepan ⅔ full of water and bring to a boil.

Add pasta and cook for 10 to 12 minutes (or as directed on package) and drain. Chop celery, onion, green or red pepper, and tomato.

In a serving bowl combine chopped vegetables, garbanzo beans, and cooked pasta. Add Parmesan cheese to Italian dressing and pour over pasta; mix well. Cover and refrigerate. Serves 10.

Pasta With Red Peppers, Greens, & Beans

4 tablespoons olive oil
1 cup chopped red onion
4 large garlic cloves, peeled and minced
6 cups fresh greens (spinach or Swiss chard), cut into ½-inch strips
3 red peppers; roasted, peeled, and coarsely chopped
16-ounce can cannelloni beans, drained and rinsed
1 teaspoon dried basil
1 teaspoon dried oregano
¼ teaspoon salt
1 pound uncooked spiral or penne pasta
¼ cup pine nuts, optional

Cook pasta according to package directions. While pasta is cooking sauté onions and olive oil in a large nonstick skillet for 3 to 4 minutes.

Add garlic and greens and continue to sauté til greens wilt.

Add red peppers, cannelloni beans, herbs, and salt.

Continue cooking til beans are heated through, 3 to 4 minutes. When pasta is cooked, drain.

Serve red pepper, greens, and bean mixture over pasta. Sprinkle with pine nuts, if desired. Serves 4.

Quick & Easy Homemade Spaghetti Sauce

¼ cup olive oil
1 garlic clove, minced
6 ounces tomato paste
28 ounces crushed tomatoes
1 tablespoon parsley
1 teaspoon basil
1 cup applesauce
Salt and pepper to taste
½ to ¾ cup grated Romano cheese

In large saucepan sauté garlic in olive oil. Add tomato paste and simmer for 15 minutes.

Add remaining ingredients, except cheese, and simmer for an additional 40 minutes. Stir in grated cheese.

Spaghetti with Zucchini & Mozzarella

8 ounces uncooked spaghetti
2 teaspoons cooking oil
2 medium shredded zucchini or 1 bunch finely chopped fresh broccoli
½ large onion, chopped
8 ounces part-skim shredded mozzarella
½ cup skim milk
¼ teaspoon salt
¼ teaspoon black pepper
¼ teaspoon basil
½ teaspoon garlic powder, optional

Fill large pot ⅔ full with water and bring to a boil.

Cook spaghetti til just tender, least amount of time per package directions.

Meanwhile, in large skillet, cook zucchini (or broccoli) and onion in oil til tender, about 7 minutes.

When spaghetti is done drain and return to pot. Add zucchini-onion mixture and remaining ingredients.

Over low heat toss spaghetti mixture til cheese is melted. Serve immediately. Serves 5.

Three-Cheese Baked Ziti

15-ounce package part-skim ricotta cheese
2 eggs, beaten
¼ cup grated Parmesan cheese
1 pound uncooked ziti, or other pasta
28-ounce jar pasta sauce
1 cup shredded part-skim mozzarella cheese
Vegetable cooking spray

Cook and drain ziti or pasta of your choice according to lowest amount of time on package directions.

Preheat oven to 350 degrees F. Combine ricotta cheese, eggs, and Parmesan cheese in medium bowl and set aside. Combine hot pasta and pasta sauce. Spray 13 x 9-inch baking dish with cooking spray.

Spoon ½ of the pasta mixture into dish, evenly top with cheese mixture, and then add remaining pasta.

Sprinkle with mozzarella cheese. Bake for 30 minutes or til heated through.

Canapés and Appetizers

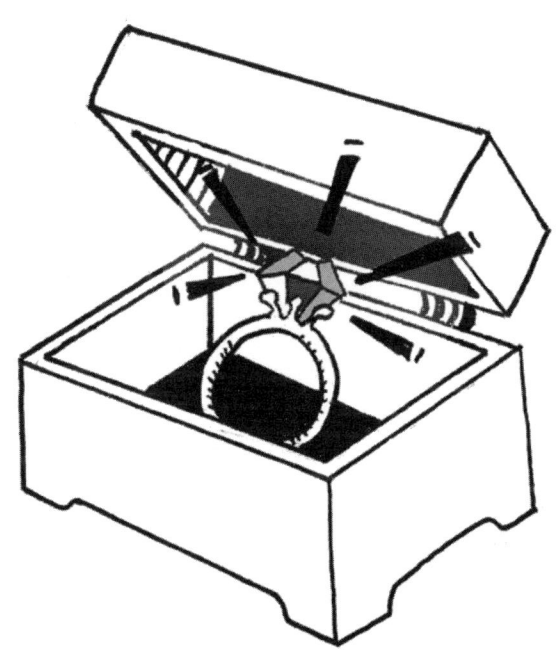

SAVORY SNEAK PREVIEW

The Engagement ◊ Coffin for a Butterfly

Becoming engaged while crowded into a car with two other couples was, to say the least, a spontaneous action on both our parts. In fact, I would be hard pressed to imagine a less romantic or more ridiculous setting. Dittie, however, said, "Yes," and that was all that really mattered.

Since the proposal was completely spontaneous, I had no engagement ring or any other token of my love to give her. I did not know how I was going to afford to buy her a ring, but summer was approaching, and I anticipated I might get a job with Standard Oil like I had the previous summer. That is the way it turned out, and I purchased the finest looking diamond ring I could afford. It was less than one carat, but I thought it was beautiful.

I had not told her I had bought her a ring when we returned to school the following autumn. I wanted to present it to her in a special way, so I decided to make a small box to put it in. I obtained some thin pieces of walnut and started cutting, sanding, and gluing pieces together. I worked on this for weeks in my spare time, even in the dorm cafeteria. One day, Dittie asked me what I was working on, and because I wanted the ring to be a surprise I hesitated with my response. My friend, Slim, quickly came up with the answer that it was a *"coffin for a butterfly."* Henceforth, that was how we referred to it.

I finally did finish the box, lined it with velvet, and presented it to her. I am still not sure if she was really surprised, but she acted well enough to convince me that she was. The "coffin" still resides in her jewelry drawer, sans velvet. It once again contains her engagement ring which is now solidly attached to her wedding ring

I consider this a prelude to our lives together, like the canapés served before a main course. Following are the canapé recipes from Dittie's cookbook:

ALMOND FINGERS

6 slices bacon, fried and crumbled
½ pound grated sharp cheddar cheese
1 chopped onion
4 ounces slivered almonds
1 cup mayonnaise
Salt and pepper to taste

Preheat oven to 400 degrees F. Mix all ingredients together in a medium bowl. Cut crust off loaf of white bread and spread mix onto bread slices.

Cut into fingers, place on greased cookie sheet, and bake for 10 minutes. Freezes well.

ANGELS IN BLANKETS

36 shrimps, peeled and precooked
18 slices bacon

Wash and dry shrimp and wrap with ½ slice of bacon. Secure with a toothpick. Refrigerate covered til just before serving time.

Preheat broiler. Broil 6 inches from heat for 3 to 4 minutes. Turn over and broil for 1 to 2 minutes longer.

ARTICHOKE DIP

1 can artichoke hearts
1 cup Parmesan cheese

Preheat oven to 350 degrees F. Blend ingredients together in a blender. Place in pie pan and bake for 30 minutes. Serve with crackers.

ARTICHOKES & MUSHROOMS

3 tablespoons lemon juice
½ cup salad oil
3 tablespoons cider vinegar
3 tablespoons olive oil
2 teaspoons salt
Dash of pepper
½ teaspoon sugar
2 garlic cloves, sliced thin
1 cup artichoke hearts, quartered
1 cup button mushrooms

Mix all ingredients together in a medium bowl. Cover and marinate for 24 to 48 hours, or longer. If there is extra marinade, add more mushrooms and artichokes.

ARTICHOKE NIBBLES

2 (6-ounce) jars marinated artichoke hearts
1 small onion, chopped fine
1 clove garlic, minced
4 eggs beaten
¼ cup fine dry bread crumbs
¼ teaspoon salt
⅛ teaspoon pepper
⅛ teaspoon oregano
⅛ teaspoon hot sauce
½ pound sharp cheddar cheese, grated
2 tablespoon parsley
1 small jar pimentos, optional

Preheat oven to 325 degrees F. Drain 1 jar artichokes, ditch juice. Drain other jar and put juice into small frying pan, add onion, garlic and sauté. Chop artichokes into quarters.

Combine eggs, crumbs, salt, pepper, oregano, and hot sauce. Stir in cheese, pimentos, and artichokes. Add onion mix. Pour into 11 x 7-inch baking dish and sprinkle with parsley. Bake for 30 minutes or til lightly browned. Cool and cut into 1-inch square pieces.

BLUE CHEESE DIP OR DRESSING

1 cup butter milk (only ½ cup for dip)
1 cup mayonnaise
1 cup sour cream
1 package dry ranch dressing mix
½ to ¾ cup crumbled blue cheese

Combine all ingredients in large bowl except blue cheese. Fold in blue cheese. Makes about 1-quart dressing.

BLUE CHEESE LOG

8 ounces cream cheese, softened
8 ounces blue cheese, softened
¼ cup butter, softened
⅔ cup chopped ripe olives
1 tablespoon chives

In a large bowl blend cream cheese, blue cheese, and butter. Stir in olives and chives. Form into a log and roll log in chopped nuts.

BLUE CHEESE WALNUT BITES

1 ½ cups flour
2 to 3 teaspoons cracked pepper
8 ounces blue cheese
¼ cup butter
1 cup chopped walnuts
2 egg yolks, slightly beaten

In a medium bowl combine flour and pepper. With a pastry blender, cut in cheese and butter. Mix should resemble coarse crumbs. Add walnuts and egg yolks. Stir til combined. Form into a ball, knead til combined. Divide dough in half.

Shape each half into logs about 9 inches long. Wrap in saran wrap and chill for at least 2 hours. Preheat oven to 425 degrees F. Cut each log into ¼-inch thick slices. Place slices 1 inch apart on un-greased baking sheet. Bake for 8 to 10 minutes or til brown. Transfer to a wire rack.

Serve warm or at room temperature. Can store tightly covered in refrigerator up to 1 week. Makes 6 dozen.

BRAUNSCHWEIGER BALL

1 pound Braunschweiger (smoked liverwurst)
2 packages green onion dip mix
1 teaspoon sugar
1 teaspoon water

Combine ingredients with a blender in large bowl. Form into 3 balls.

Spread

1 tablespoon garlic spread
6 ounces cream cheese, softened
⅛ tablespoon hot sauce
1 tablespoon salt

Melt garlic spread over medium heat and blend with cream cheese. Mix in hot sauce and milk. Frost balls with cheese mixture and chill til firm.

Braunschweiger Ball #2

1 pound Braunschweiger (smoked liverwurst)
½ cup ketchup
1 teaspoon Worcestershire sauce
Parsley flakes

Mix ingredients together in a medium bowl and form into a ball. Frost with cream cheese and garnish with additional parsley or paprika.

Brie en Croute

1 sheet frozen puff pastry
¼ cup sliced, toasted almonds, optional
¼ cup chopped fresh parsley
1 pound Brie cheese round
1 egg beaten with 1 to 2 teaspoons water (egg wash)

Thaw pastry for 20 to 30 minutes. Preheat oven to 400 degrees F.

On lightly floured surface roll out pastry to a 14-inch square. Cut off corners to make a circle. Sprinkle almonds and parsley over center of pastry circle. Top with Brie round. Brush pastry edges with egg wash. Pull up two opposite sides over each other.

Trim the two other sides 2 inches from edge of Brie round. Pull up these two sides onto the wheel. Press edges together to seal. Place seam side down on un-greased baking sheet. Brush with egg wash.

Bake for 20 minutes or til golden brown. Let stand at least 20 minutes before serving.

Burgundy Glazed Hots

1 jar burgundy wine jelly
⅓ cup prepared mustard
1 pound skinless franks cut into 1-inch pieces

Combine jelly and mustard in large skillet over medium heat. Stir til jelly is melted and mustard blended. Add franks, simmer and baste til well-glazed. Serve hot in chafing dish with toothpicks.

Camembert Canapé

8 ounces Camembert
1 package crescent rolls, use 4 pinched together

On cookie sheet place cheese on rolls and cover with dough completely, may need to roll the dough to get a good covering. Be sure there are no openings. Place in oven (per crescent roll directions). Serve hot.

Caramelized Bacon

Preheat oven to 350 degrees F. Cut strips of bacon in half. Lay on broiler pan, overlapping. Cover with brown sugar and bake for 15 to 20 minutes. Remove and roll up. Can be made ahead and reheated in oven.

Cheese & Bacon Puffs

1 cup mayonnaise
½ cup grated cheddar cheese
2 teaspoons drained horseradish
1 tablespoon Solera sherry
½ cup cooked and crumbled bacon

Combine ingredients in large bowl and spread thickly on toast cut-outs or crackers and broil til bubbly and brown. Makes 30.

CHEESE BALL

12 ounces cream cheese, softened
¼ cup mayonnaise
⅓ cup grated Parmesan cheese
⅛ teaspoon garlic
⅛ teaspoon oregano

Mix all ingredients together in large bowl. Form into 1 or 2 balls. Roll in chopped nuts and top with a cherry.

CHEESE OLIVE PUFFS

8 ounces shredded sharp cheddar cheese
1 cup flour
½ teaspoon paprika
¼ pound butter, softened
2 to 4 dozen olives

Preheat oven to 400 degrees F. Combine all ingredients in large bowl except olives. Mix well and chill. Wrap olives with mixture. Pour into 13 x 9-inch oven-proof serving dish. Bake for 15 minutes. Serve hot. May be frozen.

CHEESE SNACK ROUNDS

5-ounce jar sharp processed cheese spread
½ cup biscuit mix
3 tablespoons sesame seeds

Mix cheese spread and biscuit mix in medium bowl. Shape into 1-inch diameter roll on lightly floured board.

Roll in sesame seeds, pressing lightly if necessary.

Wrap and refrigerate at least 2 hours. Heat oven to 375 degrees F. Cut roll into ¼-inch slices.

Place on lightly greased cookie sheet. Bake til golden brown 8 to 10 minutes. Makes about 42 appetizers.

CHEESE STUFFED MUSHROOMS

20 large fresh mushrooms
Melted butter
1 package Leiderkranz cheese
2 teaspoons parsley, chopped
2 teaspoons onion, minced
2 tablespoons dry white wine
Salt and pepper to taste

Preheat oven to 375 degrees F. Remove stems from mushrooms. Finely chop enough stems to make ½ cup. Brush caps inside and out with melted butter.

Slice Leiderkranz cheese into small mixing bowl and beat til smooth. Stir in chopped stems, parsley, onion, dry white wine, salt, and pepper.

Spoon mixture into mushroom caps. Place on baking sheet and bake 15 minutes til lightly browned. Serve hot.

CHEESY CRAB DIP

½ pound Velveeta cheese
1 cup drained crab
1 stick margarine

Melt margarine and add diced Velveeta cheese and crab. Pour in serving dish. Tastes best when warm.

Chestnuts with Bacon

¼ cup salad oil
¼ cup soy sauce
2 tablespoons ketchup
1 teaspoon vinegar
¼ teaspoon pepper
2 minced garlic cloves

Mix ingredients in large bowl and marinate 1 can of water chestnuts for 1 hour. Preheat oven to 400 degrees F. Cut chestnuts so they are uniform size and wrap with ½ strip bacon. Secure with toothpick and roll in brown sugar. Place on cookie sheet and bake til brown, about 7 to 9 minutes. Can be made ahead and reheated.

Chipped Beef Fondue

8 ounces cream cheese, softened
1 cup milk
¼ cup Parmesan cheese
½ cup chopped onion
1 tablespoon butter
1 cup chipped beef
1 can mushrooms

Chop onion and mix in medium skillet over medium heat with melted butter, cook til soft. Don't brown. Blend in milk and cream cheese, onion mix, and other ingredients. Pour in serving dish. Serve warm with torn bread.

Cocktail Spread

8 ounces cream cheese, softened
½ cup sour cream
¼ cup mayonnaise
8 ounces broken shrimp, rinsed and drained
1 cup cocktail sauce
2 cups grated cheddar or mozzarella cheese
3 green onions, chopped
1 tomato, diced
1 pepper (green, red, etc.), chopped
1 cucumber, chopped

Mix first 3 ingredients together in medium bowl and spread in 12-inch dish or pie plate. Scatter shrimp over entire mixture. Add layer of sauce, followed by cheese, onions, tomatoes, peppers, and cucumbers. Cover til ready to use. Serve with crackers. A little lemon juice and Worcestershire sauce can be added.

Crab Dip

8 ounces cream cheese, softened
1 tablespoon milk
½ teaspoon cream style horseradish
¼ teaspoon salt
Dash of pepper
6 ¾ ounces crab
2 tablespoons minced onion
⅓ cup sliced almonds, toasted

Preheat oven to 375 degrees F. Combine cream cheese with milk in large bowl. Add horseradish, salt, pepper, crab meat, and onion. Spoon into oven-proof dish, sprinkle with almonds. Bake 15 minutes. Serve with party rye or rye crackers.

Crab meat Canapés

1 ½ ounces chopped crab
1 tablespoon horseradish
½ teaspoon mustard
½ teaspoon Worcestershire sauce
¾ cup mayonnaise
2 teaspoon sherry wine
3 hard boiled eggs, chopped

In large bowl combine all ingredients except 1 egg. Serve on crackers. Chop remaining egg very fine for garnish.

CRAB MEAT SANDWICHES

8 ounces cream cheese, softened
1 can crab, drained
2 tablespoons mayonnaise
2 tablespoons chili sauce
Dash of Worcestershire sauce
1 onion, chopped
6 ounces shrimp, drained

Put all ingredients in mixer and mix well. Spread on bread and cut into finger sandwiches.

CRAB MOUSSE

1 package unflavored gelatin
3 tablespoons skim milk
8 ounces cream cheese, softened
8 ounces plain non-fat yogurt
½ pound fresh lump crab
1 cup minced celery
½ cup sliced green onion
1 tablespoon lemon juice
1 teaspoon pepper
½ teaspoon horseradish

Coat 4-quart mold with cooking spray, set aside. Sprinkle gelatin over milk in a small pan.

Let stand 1 minute. Add cream cheese and cook over low heat, stirring til gelatin is dissolved and mix is smooth. Add yogurt, stir til well-blended and remove from heat.

Add crab, celery, onion, lemon juice, pepper, and horseradish. Blend well. Pour into mold, cover and chill til firm. Serve with Melba Toast (recipe page 40) or crackers.

One half of this recipe makes enough for 2 to 3 tables of bridge.

CRAB STUFFED EGGS

12 hard boiled eggs, shelled
6 ½ ounces crab

Cut shelled eggs in half lengthwise. Remove yolks and in a medium bowl mix together yolks, crab, and a spoonful of mayonnaise.

Spoon yolk and crab meat mixture into egg whites, about 1 tablespoon in each. Sprinkle salt and paprika on top.

CRISPY SQUARES

¼ cup margarine
1 ¼ teaspoon seasoning salt
4 ½ teaspoons Worcestershire sauce

Melt margarine in microwave-proof bowl and add the above. Add 8 cups of shredded wheat, rice, and/or corn cereal squares, 1 cup cocktail peanuts, and 1 cup sesame sticks. Zap on medium-high for 5 to 6 minutes, stirring every minute or so. Cool on wax paper and serve. This is enough to fill about 1 ½ empty oatmeal cereal boxes for storage (with lid).

CUCUMBER PECAN ROLL

8 ounces cream cheese, softened
1 teaspoon grated onion
2 tablespoons grated cucumber
½ cup finely chopped pecans

In a medium bowl combine cream cheese, onion, and cucumber. Form into tiny balls and roll in pecans. Refrigerate. The mixture can be spread onto finger sandwiches.

These are difficult to roll into small balls, but if you do, use a lot of pecans. Works better as one large cheese ball.

Cucumber Relish Boats

3 medium cucumbers
Salt
2 medium tomatoes, chopped
2 tablespoons white wine vinegar
2 teaspoons sugar
¾ teaspoon basil

Peel cucumbers and cut each lengthwise in half. Into a medium bowl remove seeds and some pulp from the cucumbers with a teaspoon to form a shell. Place upside-down to dry thoroughly. Place on serving dish in refrigerator. Coarsely chop cucumbers left in bowl. Stir in ¾ teaspoon salt and remaining ingredients, refrigerate. Salt cucumbers and spoon drained mixture into shells. Serve.

Dilled Garden Dip

16 ounces low-fat cottage cheese
2 tablespoons tarragon vinegar
1 tablespoon finely chopped onion
1 tablespoon dried parsley flakes
½ teaspoon dill
1 tablespoon skim milk
Pepper

Place cottage cheese and vinegar in blender and process til smooth. Combine cottage cheese mixture with green onion and remaining ingredients in medium bowl. Stir well and transfer to small bowl. Cover and chill. Serve with raw vegetables.

Dill Dip

½ pint sour cream
¾ cup mayonnaise
Dash of hot sauce
1 tablespoon grated onion
½ teaspoon pepper
1 teaspoon seasoning salt
2 teaspoons dill

Combine in a serving bowl and serve with crackers or raw vegetables. Serves 6 to 8.

Dried Beef Appetizer Pie

8 ounces cream cheese, softened
2 tablespoons milk
2 ½ ounces chipped beef, snipped
2 tablespoons minced onion
2 tablespoons chopped green pepper
⅛ teaspoon pepper

Preheat oven to 350 degrees F. Stir together ingredients in large bowl til well-combined. Add ½ cup sour cream and top with ¼ cup chopped nuts. Place in shallow baking dish. Bake for 15 minutes. Serve hot.

Egg & Crab Mold

10 to 12 hard boiled eggs
1 teaspoon garlic salt
1 teaspoon accent
1 teaspoon sweet soy seasoning
1 drop hot sauce
1 tablespoon Dijon mustard
½ cup mayonnaise
2 cups sour cream, beaten
2 cups crab or small shrimp

Put eggs through fine sieve or ricer. Add garlic, accent, sweet soy seasoning, hot sauce, mustard, and mayonnaise and mix in large bowl til well-blended. This should be a thick consistency. Put into a well-greased 1-quart ring mold, cover, and refrigerate til firm. Remove and turn onto plate and frost with sour cream. Fill center of mold with crab or shrimp. Garnish mold with parsley. Serve with rye crackers.

Grand Marnier Dip

1 small container whipped topping
3 ounces cream cheese, softened
4 tablespoons powdered sugar
4 tablespoons concentrated orange juice
4 tablespoons Grand Marnier
1 tablespoon honey

Blend cream cheese in large bowl til fluffy. Add whipped topping and other ingredients and chill. Serve with fruit slices. Can be refrozen.

Guacamole

2 large ripe avocados
2 teaspoons each lemon juice, lime juice, and vinegar mixed together
1 teaspoon sugar
1 tablespoon mayonnaise
2 ounces chopped green chilies
½ teaspoon coriander
¼ cucumber
⅛ onion
Salt and pepper to taste

Chop cucumber and onion very fine and add salt and pepper to taste.

Add 1 large tomato chopped into bite-size pieces. Peel and mash avocado (I suggest using a pastry cutter for this job). Add lemon, lime, vinegar, and sugar.

Add mayonnaise, chilies, coriander, cucumber, and onion. Add salt and pepper to taste. Fold in tomato. Usually enough for 4 people, but does not keep well in refrigerator.

Ham & Cheese Appetizers

2 cups biscuit mix
¾ cup finely chopped cooked ham
1 cup shredded Swiss or cheddar cheese
½ cup finely chopped onion
½ cup grated Parmesan cheese
¼ cup sour cream
2 tablespoons parsley
½ teaspoon salt
2 cloves garlic, crushed
⅔ cup milk
1 egg

Preheat oven to 350 degrees F. Grease 13 x 9-inch pan. Mix all ingredients in large bowl and spread in pan. Bake til golden brown, 25 to 30 minutes. Cut into rectangles. Makes about 36.

Ham Balls

3 cups biscuit mix
1 ½ cup finely chopped cooked ham
4 cups shredded cheddar cheese
½ cup grated Parmesan cheese
2 tablespoons parsley flakes
2 teaspoons prepared spicy mustard
⅔ cup milk

Preheat oven to 350 degrees F. Lightly grease jellyroll pan. Mix all ingredients in large bowl til well-combined. Shape into 1-inch balls.

Place about 2 inches apart on cookie sheet. Bake 20 to 25 minutes or til brown. Immediately remove from pan. Serve warm.

HAUTE GARLIC BREAD

Preheat oven to 350 degrees F. Cut rough, country style bread into ¾-inch slices. Brush both sides with a little olive oil. Toast on cookie sheet and flip once so both sides turn golden brown. Immediately rub the hot bread with whole peeled cloves of garlic.

Doll it up with a smear of Gorgonzola cheese, mashed and mixed with chopped walnuts. Top with a slice of apple or a slice of ripe tomato. Garnish with cracked pepper and a little mint for color.

HONEY CHICKEN WINGS

2 pounds chicken wings
¼ cup corn oil
¼ cup soy sauce
¼ cup orange juice
¼ cup honey
2 cloves garlic, peeled and halved
1 bunch scallions cut into 2-inch pieces
1 teaspoon accent
½ teaspoon ginger

Heat oil in a large skillet over medium heat. Add chicken and brown on all sides. Drain excess fat and heat. Add soy, orange juice, honey, garlic, scallions, accent, and ginger.

Stir in wings til coated. Simmer covered for 40 minutes turning occasionally.

Remove lid, increase heat, and cook til liquid is evaporated and wings are glazed, about 5 minutes. Remove garlic. Can be frozen and reheated in oven on broiler pan (line bottom with foil).

HOT & GOOD!

½ cup mayonnaise
8 ounces grated sharp cheddar cheese
1 small can chopped ripe olives
4 green onions, chopped fine
¾ teaspoon curry
8 English muffins

Preheat oven to 400 degrees F. Mix all ingredients in medium bowl and spread on split muffins. Bake for 8 minutes. Allow to stand a few minutes and then cut each muffin half into 4 pieces

HOT ASPARAGUS CANAPÉS

20 slices thin white bread
3 ounces blue cheese, softened
8 ounces cream cheese, softened
1 egg
20 spears cooked or canned asparagus
½ pound melted butter

Trim crust off bread and roll slices thin. Blend cheeses and egg in small bowl to workable consistency and spread evenly on each slice of bread.

Place asparagus on top and roll up, using toothpick to fasten. Dip in butter to coat thoroughly.

Place rolls on cookie sheet and freeze. When frozen firmly slice into 3 equal pieces. When ready to serve bake in preheated 400 degree F oven for 15 minutes, or til lightly brown. Serve hot.

Hot Parmesan Snacks

1 cup mayonnaise
⅓ cup grated Parmesan cheese
1 teaspoon Worcestershire sauce
¼ teaspoon onion salt
1 tablespoon sherry
Butter crackers

Combine all ingredients in medium bowl and spread thickly on butter crackers and broil til brown, about 4 minutes. Serve hot.

Impossible Quiche

12 slices bacon, fried crisp and crumbled
1 cup shredded Swiss cheese
⅓ cup finely chopped onion
2 cups milk
½ cup biscuit mix
4 eggs
¼ teaspoon salt
¼ teaspoon pepper

Preheat oven to 300 degrees F. Grease 8 x 8-inch baking pan. Sprinkle bacon, cheese, and onion evenly over bottom of pan.

Place remaining ingredients in blender. Cover and blend on high for 1 minute and pour in pan.

Bake til golden brown and an inserted knife comes out clean, 50 to 55 minutes. Let stand 5 minutes before cutting.

Italian Party Bites

12-inch Italian bread shell
1 tablespoon olive oil
1 teaspoon Italian seasoning
1 teaspoon minced onion
½ teaspoon thyme leaves
½ cup shredded mozzarella cheese
1 cup thinly sliced vegetables; red peppers, zucchini, mushrooms, or onion
1 can sliced black olives, drained
¼ cup shredded Parmesan cheese

Preheat oven to 450 degrees F. Place bread shell on cookie sheet. In large bowl toss together next 6 ingredients. Spread mixture over bread shell.

Top with olives and cheese. Bake 8 to 10 minutes. Cut into 2-inch squares.

Layered Shrimp Dip

3 ounces cream cheese, softened
6 tablespoons salsa, divided
½ cup cocktail sauce
18 ounces canned small shrimp, drained and rinsed
2 ¼ ounces ripe olives, sliced and drained
4 ounces shredded cheddar cheese
4 ounces shredded jack cheese
1 small onion, sliced

Combine cream cheese and 3 tablespoons salsa in small bowl and spread in un-greased 9-inch pie pan. Combine cocktail sauce and remaining salsa and spread over cream cheese.

Place shrimp evenly over top. Sprinkle with olives. Combine cheeses and sprinkle over olives. Top with onion. Chill. Serve with tortilla chips.

Lobster Dip

2 finely chopped lobster tails
4 tablespoons mayonnaise
1 tablespoon lemon juice
6 ounces cream cheese, softened
1 tablespoon chives
4 to 5 tablespoons sliced olives

Mix all ingredients together in large bowl and spoon into serving dish. Use crackers or torn-up bread to dip with.

Marinated Mushrooms

¼ cup sherry wine vinegar
¼ teaspoon paprika
⅔ cup olive oil
2 large shallots
2 cups sliced mushrooms

Mix together all ingredients in large container and marinate mushrooms for 1 or more hours. Sprinkle with diced water chestnuts. Serve at room temperature.

Mushroom Roll-ups

Preheat oven to 350 degrees F. Slice crust off thin bread and roll with rolling pin til very thin. Spread with condensed mushroom soup and roll up. Wrap in ½ slice bacon and freeze.

Cut into 4 pieces while still frozen and cook about 15 minutes. Serve hot.

1 loaf bread = 1 can soup

Marinated Cucumbers

½ cup vinegar
½ cup sugar
½ cup water

Combine in small pan and heat til sugar dissolves. Peel cucumber and thinly slice it into a bowl and cover with hot mixture. Cover and refrigerate at least 5 hours, overnight is better. Serve as canapé, small side salad, or as a garnish. Keeps well in fridge.

Pepperoni Bread

1 package pizza dough
4 ounces provolone cheese, sliced thin
4 ounces pepperoni, sliced thin
1 sweet onion, sliced thin
5 green peppers, sliced thin
1 clove garlic, chopped
Parmesan cheese, grated

Preheat oven to 325 degrees F. In large skillet sauté onion, garlic, and green pepper in 1 tablespoon of olive oil til soft.

Roll out pizza dough as thin as desired (approximately ½ of its original thickness). Place pepperoni all over, touching sides up to ½-inch from edge.

Layer cheese over pepperoni and spread green pepper mixture over cheese. Sprinkle with Parmesan cheese. Roll dough snuggly like a jellyroll.

Place on cookie sheet with seam side down. Brush with egg white. Bake for 25 to 30 minutes. Can freeze after baking.

Piña Colada Dip

Mix coconut cream instant pudding with 8 ½ ounces pineapple juice, ½ cup sour cream, 1 cup whipped topping, and 1 jigger of rum. Serve with fruit slices.

Pizza Quiche

9-inch unbaked pie shell
⅔ cup shredded Swiss or cheddar cheese
1 tablespoon minced onion
3 eggs
2 tablespoon flour
1 cup milk
8-ounce can tomato sauce with mushrooms
½ teaspoon salt
¼ teaspoon basil
¼ teaspoon oregano

Preheat oven to 400 degrees F. Bake shell for 5 minutes. Remove from oven and cover with cheese. Sprinkle in minced onion. Beat eggs and flour til smooth.

In large bowl blend in milk, ½ cup tomato sauce, salt, and other herbs. Pour into pie shell. Bake at 400 degrees F for 15 minutes then reduce heat to 325 degrees F and continue to bake for 25 to 30 minutes.

Remove from oven and drizzle remaining sauce in spoke design on top. Let stand 10 minutes before cutting.

Rye Bread Dip

1 ½ pints sour cream
3 tablespoons parsley flakes
3 teaspoons beau monde seasoning salt
1 ½ pints mayonnaise
2 teaspoon dill weed
2 tablespoons minced onion
6 ounces corned beef, shredded
Round rye bread loaf

Cut off top of rye bread loaf. Pull out insides of loaf and tear insides and top into bite-size pieces to use as dippers.

In large bowl combine all ingredients and pour into prepared round rye bread loaf.

This recipe will fill 1 round rye loaf twice, or you can make 2 separate loaves. Serves 12 to 15.

Sausage Biscuit

1 pound hot ground sausage
2 cups biscuit mix
2 cups grated cheddar cheese

Preheat oven to 350 degrees. In large skillet over medium heat brown sausage and pour off grease and add cheese to sausage til melted. Pour into a bowl. Add biscuit mix and stir.

Roll into 1-inch balls, place on cookie sheet, and bake for 10 to 12 minutes. Makes about 36 balls. May be stored in freezer before baking.

Sausage Rye Canapés

1 pound ground beef
1 pound ground sausage
1 pound Velveeta cheese

Preheat oven to 350 degrees F. In large skillet over medium heat brown beef and sausage. Drain and melt in the cheese. Place a spoonful on party rye slices. Bake for 20 minutes. Serve hot. May be kept frozen til ready to bake and serve.

Sausage Snack Wraps

2 (8-ounce) cans crescent rolls
48 fully cooked small smoked sausage links

Preheat oven to 375 degrees F. Separate dough into 8 triangles. Cut each triangle length wise into thirds. Place sausage on shortest side of each triangle.

Roll up from short side to opposite point. Bake on un-greased cookie sheet for 12 to 15 minutes or til golden brown. To make ahead, prepare, cover, and refrigerate up to 2 hours before baking. Serve hot with Dijon mustard.

Scallops Seviche

1 pound raw scallops
Lemon or lime juice
2 ripe, seeded tomatoes
Green onions
Ripe avocado, firm
Small can chopped green chilies
Salt and/or liquid hot pepper

Chop scallops. In large bowl cover scallops with lemon or lime juice and let stand for a couple of hours til they lose their translucence.

Drain and add chopped tomatoes, chopped green onions, chopped avocado, and chopped green chilies.

Season to taste with salt and/or liquid hot pepper. Spoon into serving dish and serve chilled with crackers.

Sherry Potato Chip Dip

1 large can deviled ham
8 ounces cream cheese, softened
1 teaspoon Worcestershire sauce
⅓ cup sherry wine

In large bowl beat cream cheese. Add ham and Worcestershire sauce. Add sherry last. Beat slowly for 3 to 5 minutes. Serve with chips or crackers. Serves 8 to 10.

Shrimp Dip

8 ounces cream cheese, softened
1 teaspoon lemon juice
Garlic powder to taste
Paprika to taste
1 can cream of shrimp soup

Blend cream cheese, lemon juice, dash of garlic powder, and paprika. Blend in cream of shrimp soup. Do not over beat as this makes mixture too thin. Chill. Add small shrimp, if desired.

Shrimp Spread

8 ounces canned shrimp, rinsed and drained
3 ounces cream cheese, softened
2 teaspoons sour cream
2 teaspoons lemon juice
1 teaspoon Dijon mustard
½ teaspoon hot pepper sauce

Chop shrimp fine and in large bowl combine remainder of ingredients til well-blended. Chill 8 hours or overnight. Serve cool with crackers.

Shrimp Toast

8 ounces shrimp, drained
4 water chestnuts, finely minced
1 egg slightly beaten
1 teaspoon salt
6 slices day old bread
1 teaspoon cream sherry
1 tablespoon cornstarch
2 cups vegetable oil

Chop shrimp til very fine. In large bowl add chestnuts, salt, sugar, sherry, cornstarch, and egg. Trim crust from bread and cut into 4 triangles. Spread a teaspoon of shrimp mix over each. Heat oil to 375 degrees F. In large skillet place triangles shrimp side down in hot oil. Fry about 1 minute til edges are slightly brown. Turn and fry on other side for ½ minute. Drain well. Serve warm or wrap and freeze. When ready to use, preheat oven to 400 degrees F and bake for 10 to 12 minutes.

Stuffed Cherry Tomatoes

1 basket cherry tomatoes
1 large ripe avocado
4 teaspoons lemon juice
1 teaspoon minced onion
1 garlic clove, minced
½ teaspoon salt
6 slices bacon, fried and crumbled

Wash and stem 1 basket cherry tomatoes. Cut each in half and scoop out seeds. Lay cut side down and drain on towel for about 30 minutes.

Guacamole Stuffing

Peel and remove pit from avocado. Mash shell coarsely with fork or cut fine. Toss in large bowl and stir in lemon juice, onion, garlic, and salt. Also fry bacon til crisp. Drain and then crumble. Fill tomatoes with guacamole, sprinkle with bacon. Makes about 40.

Stuffed Cukes

Peel and cut out centers of cucumbers. Allow to drain and dry slightly. Fill with cream cheese and sprinkle with chives or nuts. Chill and cut into slices. Serve placed on crackers. 1 cucumber = about 40 appetizers.

Stuffed Mushrooms

Take washed mushroom caps and stuff with seasoned bulk sausage. Broil at lowest shelf of oven for 15 to 20 minutes.

Swedish Meatballs

1 ½ cups ketchup
1 cup water
½ cup vinegar
4 tablespoons packed brown sugar
6 drops hot sauce
4 tablespoons freshly minced onions
4 tablespoons Worcestershire
3 teaspoons salt
2 teaspoons dry mustard

Mix sauce ingredients and simmer sauce 30 minutes to 1 hour with meatballs.

Sweet & Sour Kielbasa

1 kielbasa ring
1 small jar grape jelly
1 bottle chili sauce

In large skillet brown kielbasa over medium heat for 5 minutes and cut into diagonal slices. Bring jelly and chili sauce to a boil. Drop meat into sauce. Let simmer about 30 minutes.

TACO DIP

Spread 1 can bean dip on bottom of pie pan. In bowl mix together 16 ounces sour cream and 2 cans chopped green chilies, layer on bean dip. Add 1 finely chopped avocado and 2 cloves finely chopped garlic. Garnish with chopped tomatoes, diced scallions, and chopped black olives. Serve with tortilla chips. Serves 10 to 12.

THREE-CHEESE BALL

4 ounces cream cheese, softened
4 ounces cheddar cheese
4 ounces shredded blue cheese
1 tablespoon minced onion
1 tablespoon Worcestershire sauce
½ cup chopped walnuts

Place all ingredients, except nuts, in mixing bowl. Whip til ingredients are combined. Shape into a ball and roll in chopped nuts. Wrap in wax paper and refrigerate til chilled.

THREE-CHEESE SPREAD

4 ounces each cream cheese, softened
4 ounces blue cheese spread
4 ounces cheddar cheese spread

Bring cheeses to room temperature. In large bowl mix cheese thoroughly. Place in serving dish and serve with Melba Toast (recipe below) or crackers. Also good on celery sticks.

MELBA TOAST

Preheat oven, about 225 to 250 degrees F. Using very thin-sliced bread, cut slices in quarters from corner to corner. Lay the pieces in a single layer on a cookie sheet. Place them in oven and bake til they turn lightly brown (about 1 hour). Turn off the oven and allow the toast to cool in oven. Store in an airtight container and it will stay fresh for several weeks.

TOMATO-MUSHROOM CANAPÉ

2 pounds medium mushrooms (about 34)
4 ounces blue cheese
1 tablespoon minced green onion
1 teaspoon Worcestershire sauce
¾ pint cherry tomatoes cut in half (about 17)

Preheat oven to 375 degrees F. Remove mushroom stems and place caps in a 13 x 9-inch baking dish. Blend blue cheese, onion, and Worcestershire. Fill mushroom caps with ¼ teaspoon bread crumbs and then ½ teaspoon of cheese mixture. Top each with tomato half. Bake for 15 to 20 minutes. Cheese will melt in oven.

VEGGIE PIZZA

16 ounces cream cheese, softened
1 package ranch dressing mix
1 cup mayonnaise
2 packages crescent rolls

In bowl combine first 3 ingredients. Unroll crescents and place on 15 x 11-inch jellyroll pan and bake as directed. Cool and spread with cream cheese mixture. Cut into slices and decorate with veggies.

ZUCCHINI HORS D'OEUVRES

3 cups thinly cubed zucchini
1 cup biscuit mix
½ cup chopped onion
¾ cup grated Parmesan cheese
2 tablespoons parsley
½ cup vegetable oil
4 eggs, slightly beaten
½ teaspoon garlic

Preheat oven to 350 degrees F. Combine ingredients and pour into greased 13 x 9-inch pan, season with salt and pepper. Bake for 35 minutes. Let set before cutting.

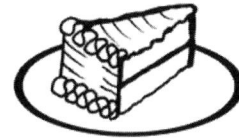

Desserts

DESSERT DILEMMA

Dinner at Persutti's ◇ Do Not Forget Dessert

The girl's dormitory cafeteria was great, but they did not provide meals on Sunday evening. Thus, of course, we were on our own for the evening. I remember one time when four couples of us decided to go to Persutti's, one of our favorite Italian restaurants. So the eight of us piled into Dave's car (the only one of the group who had a car) and off we went.

We settled ourselves at the designated table, perused the extensive menu, and ordered our choices. During the ensuing chit-chat while waiting for our dinners, we gradually discovered that the ladies had understood the guys were buying; on the other hand, the guys had tacitly assumed the outing was Dutch treat.

Having finally discovered the true state of affairs, we each cleaned our pockets or purses of everything that resembled cash money and pooled it in the middle of the table. There was no such thing as credit cards in the 1940s, only cash or personal checks.

Our dinners arrived and I know that I, for one, wondered why I had not ordered something less expensive. Although not expressed aloud, this thought was probably lurking in each mind. It hardly needs to be said that we all declined the suggestion of dessert. While waiting for the tab we sort of discussed the possibilities of any extra money we might have back in our rooms; maybe a check from Mom or Dad we had not yet cashed; who we knew who might have a few bucks to lend; etc.

The bill finally arrived. The waitress placed it in front of one of the guys and discretely backed away while Chuck examined it. He stared at it for a couple of seconds (which almost seemed like minutes to the rest of us), looked up and said, "Yipe!"

The net result was that the waitress received a tip of approximately thirty-seven cents that evening. We had been financially solvent after all.

Although we had no desserts that evening, you need not do without. You might want to sample some of the following items:

APPLE BUNDT CAKE

3 cups flour
2 cups sugar
1 cup chopped pecans
1 ½ cups cooking oil
4 cups diced apples
3 eggs
½ teaspoon salt
1 teaspoon baking soda
1 teaspoon vanilla extract
Powdered sugar

Preheat oven to 350 degrees F. Mix dry ingredients in a large bowl and add the remaining wet ingredients. Beat for 4 minutes on medium speed. Pour into well-greased bundt pan. Bake for 45 minutes. Dust top with powdered sugar. Serves about 8.

APPLE CHEESE PIE

⅓ cup sugar
⅓ cup butter, softened
1 tablespoon shortening
¼ teaspoon vanilla extract
1 cup flour
⅛ teaspoon salt
16 ounces cream cheese, softened
½ cup sugar
¼ teaspoon vanilla extract
2 eggs
1 teaspoon cinnamon
¼ cup sliced almonds
4 cups Granny Smith apples, peeled and sliced

Preheat oven to 450 degrees F. In large bowl beat sugar, butter, shortening, and vanilla extract together til creamy. Add flour and salt and pat into 9-inch pie pan. Place apples in single layer in shallow baking pan. Cover with foil and bake for 15 minutes.

Filling

Reduce heat to 400 degrees F. In large bowl beat cream cheese, ½ cup sugar, and ½ teaspoon vanilla extract til fluffy. Add eggs all at once. Beat at low speed til combined.

Pour into dough lined pie pan. Arrange apples on top. Combine ⅓ cup sugar and cinnamon. Sprinkle over top of filling along with almonds. Bake for 40 minutes. Serves 8.

APRICOT NUT BARS

½ cup butter, softened
½ cup packed brown sugar
1 cup sifted flour
¼ teaspoon baking soda
½ teaspoon salt
1 ½ cups rolled oats
1 cup apricot preserves
¼ cup chopped nuts

Preheat oven to 350 degrees F. Grease 9 x 9-inch baking pan. Beat butter and brown sugar in medium bowl til fluffy.

In separate bowl sift flour, baking soda, and salt together. Stir into butter-sugar mixture. Add oats and blend thoroughly. Press ⅔ of mixture over bottom of prepared pan. Combine apricot preserves and nuts. Spread evenly over surface of crumb mixture.

Sprinkle with remaining ⅓ crumb mixture, patting slightly onto filling. Bake 30 minutes or til lightly browned. For cookies cut into bars while still slightly warm.

For a dessert cut into squares. Serve topped with whipped cream, if desired. Makes 2 dozen cookies or 9 squares.

BAKED PEACHES FOR TWO

4 canned peach halves, drained
2 tablespoons chopped walnuts
2 tablespoons packed brown sugar
½ teaspoon grated orange peel
⅛ teaspoon allspice

Preheat oven to 350 degrees F. Place peaches in small baking dish, cut side up. In small bowl combine nuts, brown sugar, orange peel, and allspice. Sprinkle over peaches and bake for 20 minutes. Serve with ice cream. Serves 2.

BAKED PEARS WITH MARSALA

1 medium size lemon
8 medium firm Bosc pears
2 teaspoons plus ⅓ cup sugar
½ cup sweet Marsala wine
2 tablespoons melted butter

Preheat oven to 450 degrees F. With vegetable peeler, remove peel from lemon in 2 ½-inch by ½-inch strips. Squeeze juice from lemon.

With apple corer, remove cores from blossom end of unpeeled pears, but do not remove stems. With pastry brush, brush insides of pears with lemon juice and sprinkle insides with 2 teaspoons sugar.

In shallow 1 ½ to 2-quart baking dish, mix lemon-peel strips, Marsala wine, and ⅓ cup water. Place ⅓ cup sugar on sheet of waxed paper.

With pastry brush, brush pears with melted butter and roll in sugar to coat. Place pears, cored end down, in baking dish. Sprinkle sugar that is left on waxed paper into baking dish.

Bake pears 40 to 50 minutes til fork-tender, basting occasionally with syrup in dish.

Cool pears slightly, but serve warm. Or cool completely, cover and refrigerate up to 1 day ahead. Reheat pears to serve warm later. Serves 8.

BLITZ TORTE

1 cup flour
1 teaspoon baking powder
⅛ teaspoon salt
½ cup shortening
4 eggs, separated
1 teaspoon vanilla extract
3 tablespoons milk
½ cup blanched sliced almonds
1 tablespoon sugar
½ teaspoon cinnamon

Preheat oven to 350 degrees F. In large bowl sift flour, salt, and baking powder. In separate bowl beat shortening and ½ cup sugar til fluffy. Add egg yolks, vanilla extract, milk, and then the dry ingredients.

Spread mix in two 8-inch greased round pans.

Beat egg whites and add remaining sugar. Spread over other mix. Sprinkle sugar, cinnamon, and almonds over cake.

Bake for 20 to 25 minutes. Top with whipped cream. Serves 6 to 8.

BLACK FOREST TORTE

1 package fudge brownie mix (20 to 24 ounces)
21 ounces can cherry pie filling
¼ teaspoon almond extract
4 ounces whipped topping

Preheat oven to 350 degrees F. Grease bottom of 10-inch spring form pan. Prepare brownie mix as directed, but bake in spring form pan for 40 to 50 minutes or til inserted toothpick comes out clean. Cool completely in pan.

When brownies are cool, remove sides and bottom of spring form pan and place on cake dish. Spread pie filling on top of brownies, leaving ¼-inch border around edge. With rubber spatula, gently fold almond extract into whipped topping. Spoon whipped topping into decorating bag and with large rosette tube, pipe pretty design around edge. Serves 15 to 18.

BLUEBERRY TORTE

1 ½ cup vanilla cookie crumbs
¾ stick melted margarine

Preheat oven to 375 degrees F. Mix and blend cookie crumbs and margarine together til crumbly. Press into bottom of tart pan with removable bottom. Bake for 15 minutes.

8 ounces cream cheese, softened
2 eggs
½ cup sugar
1 tablespoon vanilla extract
2 teaspoons lemon zest

Preheat oven to 375 degrees F. In large bowl blend cream cheese, sugar, and eggs with beater. Mix in vanilla extract and lemon zest. Pour batter into cookie crumb crust. Bake 25 to 30 minutes. Cool.

2 cups blueberries, frozen and thawed, save juice
2 tablespoons cornstarch

In a saucepan combine blueberry juice, ¼ cup sugar, ¼ teaspoon salt, and cornstarch. Cook over low heat til thick. Then add blueberries and pour in crust.

Glaze

1 tablespoon lemon juice
1 cup currant jelly

Combine and pour over fruit. Serves 4.

BUTTERSCOTCH CHEESE CAKE

Crust

2 cups graham cracker crumbs
2 tablespoons flour
2 tablespoons sugar
½ stick unsalted margarine

Preheat oven to 325 degrees F. Combine ingredients til crumbly and bake in a spring form pan for 15 minutes.

Filling

12 ounces butterscotch chips
¼ cup heavy cream

In double boiler melt filling ingredients and beat til smooth. Cool slightly. Add 16 ounces cream cheese and whip well. Add ½ cup brown sugar, 4 eggs (1 at a time), and 1 cup sour cream. Beat til smooth. Add flour and vanilla extract and fold into butterscotch mixture. Blend well. Pour into crust. Bake at 325 degrees F for 1 hour over water bath. Leave in oven for 1 hour. Garnish with butterscotch sauce and toffee bar crumbs. Serves 8 to 10.

Caramel Peach Crunch

½ cup flour
1 cup uncooked oats
¾ cup packed brown sugar
1 teaspoon cinnamon
½ teaspoon salt
½ cup butter, melted
1 can sliced peaches, drained
½ gallon vanilla ice cream

Preheat oven to 400 degrees F. In large bowl combine flour, oats, sugar, cinnamon, and salt. Add butter and mix well. In a 9-inch pie pan arrange peaches over bottom and sprinkle oat mixture over top. Bake 25 to 30 minutes. Serve warm over ice cream. Serves 4 to 6.

Cheese Cake

1 package yellow cake mix
8 ounces cream cheese, softened
½ cup sugar
15-ounce can fruit filling; blueberry, cherry
1 ½ cup milk
3 tablespoons lemon juice
3 teaspoons vanilla extract
4 eggs

Preheat oven to 300 degrees F. Reserve 1 cup cake mix. In large bowl combine remaining cake mix, 1 egg, and oil til crumbly. Press crust mixture evenly in bottom and ¾ up the side of greased 13 x 9-inch pan. In same bowl blend cream cheese and sugar. Add 3 eggs and reserved cake mix and beat 1 minute at medium speed. At low speed add milk and flavoring and mix til smooth. Pour into crust.

Bake for 45 to 55 minutes til center is firm. When cool, top with fruit filling and chill before serving. Store in refrigerator. Can use two 9-inch pans for 40 to 50 minutes. Serves 10.

Cherry Pudding

½ cup sugar
½ cup milk
1 teaspoon baking powder
2 to 3 tablespoons butter, softened
1 cup flour
1 ½ cups tart pie cherries, packed in water
1 cup sugar
1 cup water

Preheat oven to 375 degrees F. In large bowl mix ½ cup sugar, milk, baking powder, butter, and flour together. Pour into an 8 x 8-inch square pan. Mix 1 cup sugar and water in medium saucepan. Bring to a boil and continue to boil til sugar dissolves. Add cherries and gently pour over cake mixture. Bake for 45 minutes or til brown. Serves 6 to 9.

Chocolate Angel Pie

2 egg whites
⅛ teaspoon salt
⅛ teaspoon cream of tartar
½ cup sifted sugar
½ cup finely chopped nuts
½ teaspoon vanilla extract
1 package German sweet chocolate
3 tablespoons water
1 teaspoon vanilla extract
1 cup whipped cream

Preheat oven to 300 degrees F. In medium mixing bowl beat egg whites with salt and cream of tartar til foamy. Add sugar gradually, beating til very stiff. Fold in nuts and ½ teaspoon vanilla extract. Spread in greased 8-inch pie pan, building up at sides. Bake for 50 to 55 minutes. Allow to cool.

Melt chocolate in water over low heat, stirring constantly. Cool til mixture thickens. Add 1 teaspoon vanilla extract and fold into whipped cream. Pile into meringue shell and chill for 2 hours.

Chocolate Crispy Ice Cream Pie

1 cake German sweet chocolate
2 tablespoons butter

Melt the above in double boiler and add 2 cups rice cereal. Line 10-inch pie pan and place in refrigerator.

Fill with ice cream and top with grated chocolate. Good with vanilla or mint chocolate chip ice cream. Serves 8 to 10.

Coconut Torte

1 cup graham cracker crumbs
½ cup coconut flakes
½ cup chopped walnuts
4 egg whites
¼ teaspoon salt
1 teaspoon vanilla extract
1 cup sugar

Preheat oven to 350 degrees F. In mixing bowl combine graham cracker crumbs, coconut, and nuts. Beat egg whites, salt, and vanilla extract til soft peaks form.

Gradually add sugar and beat til stiff peaks form.

Fold in graham cracker mixture. Spread in well-greased 10-inch pie pan. Bake for 30 minutes. When cool, top with ice cream. Serves 8 to 10.

Cream Cheese Tarts

1 ¼ cup graham cracker crumbs
16 ounces cream cheese, softened
3 eggs, separated
¾ cup sugar
1 cup sour cream
1 teaspoon vanilla extract
2 tablespoons sugar
60 candied cherries

Preheat oven to 350 degrees F. Butter mini muffin tins (1 ¼-inch bottom x 1 ¾-inch top). Place 1 tablespoon of graham cracker crumbs into each cup.

Press down with finger to compact crumbs in bottom of cups. Mix cream cheese, egg yolks, and ¾ cup sugar. In separate bowl beat egg whites til fluffy and add the above.

Put 1 teaspoon of cream cheese mixture into each cup. Bake for 15 minutes. Remove from oven. Allow to cool.

In medium bowl mix sour cream, 2 tablespoons sugar, and vanilla extract. Place dab of mixture on each cup. Return to oven. Bake 5 minutes more. Cool and decorate with cherries. Makes 60 tarts.

Date Pudding

1 cup packed brown sugar
1 tablespoon butter, softened
1 cup flour
½ teaspoon cinnamon
½ teaspoon vanilla extract
1 cup dates
½ cup chopped nuts
½ cup milk
2 teaspoons baking powder

In large bowl mix above ingredients together. In large saucepan boil 1 cup brown sugar and 2 to 2 ¼ cups water.

Put syrup in oblong pan and drop batter in syrup. Bake 30 minutes. Serve with whipped cream. Serves 4.

FOOD FOR THE ANGELS

2 egg whites
25 butter crackers, crushed
1 teaspoon vanilla extract
1 cup whipped topping
¾ cup sugar
½ cup walnuts
4-ounce can grated coconut

Preheat oven to 350 degrees F. In large mixing bowl beat egg whites til stiff. Fold in sugar and crackers to form crumbs. Add nuts and vanilla extract and blend. Turn into greased 8-inch square pan.

Bake for 20 minutes. Spread whipped topping on top when cooled. Top with coconut. Refrigerate overnight. Serves 4 to 6.

FROSTY MINT ICE CREAM PIE

Pie shells

1 package devil's food, dark chocolate, or chocolate mint cake mix
¾ cup chocolate fudge frosting
¾ cup water
¼ cup oil

Filling

6 cups mint chocolate chip or your favorite ice cream softened

Preheat oven to 350 degrees F. Generously grease bottom, sides, and rim of two 9-inch pie pans or round cake pans. In large bowl blend all pie shell ingredients at low speed til moistened. Then beat 2 minutes on high. Spread half of batter in bottom of each pan. Do not spread up sides of pan. Bake 25 to 30 minutes. Do not over bake. Cool completely. In large bowl blend ice cream til smooth. Spread evenly in center of each shell leaving a ½-inch rim.

Heat remaining frosting just til softened, if desired. Drop by spoonfuls on top of ice cream and swirl with knife. Freeze for at least 2 hours. Store in freezer wrap airtight. Makes 2 pies and serves 12.

FROZEN GRASSHOPPER PIE

3 tablespoons margarine
24 crushed chocolate wafers
20 marshmallows
1 cup grasshopper mix
1 cup whipped heavy cream

Combine margarine and wafers til crumbly and press in 9-inch pie pan. In saucepan melt marshmallows mixed with grasshopper mix over very low heat. Cool and then mix til smooth. Fold into whipped cream, pour in shell, and freeze. Serves 8.

FRUIT COCKTAIL DESSERT

1 cup flour
1 cup sugar
1 teaspoon baking soda
Pinch of salt
1 egg
1 small can fruit cocktail
½ cup chopped nuts

Preheat oven to 325 degrees F. In large bowl sift the first four ingredients together and add the rest. Mix well and pour in greased pan.

Topping

4 tablespoons packed brown sugar
1 teaspoon butter

Mix together til crumbly and sprinkle on top of batter. Bake for 1 hour. Serves 8 to 10.

GIRL SCOUT REFRIGERATOR CAKE

2 dozen vanilla wafer cookies
½ pound sweet chocolate
3 tablespoons water
4 egg yolks
3 tablespoons sugar
⅛ teaspoon salt
4 egg whites
1 cup whipped cream
½ cup powdered sugar
½ teaspoon vanilla extract

Line bottom of loaf pan with wax paper and then line with cookies. Melt chocolate in double boiler. In large bowl combine water, beaten yolks, salt, sugar, and melted chocolate.

In large saucepan over low heat cook and stir mixture til smooth, and then cool. Beat egg whites til stiff and fold into chilled chocolate mixture.

Fill pan with alternate layers of cookies and chocolate. Cover with wax paper and refrigerate 12 to 42 hours. Serve with whipped cream. Serves 8 to 10.

GRASSHOPPER CREAM

½ cup milk
24 marshmallows
1 cup heavy cream, whipped
3 tablespoons crème de menthe
3 tablespoons crème de cocoa

Heat milk and marshmallows in double boiler, stir til smooth, and then cool completely.

In small bowl combine whipped cream, crème de menthe, and crème de cocoa. Fold into cooled marshmallow mixture. Serves 4 to 6.

LEMON BARS

½ cup butter, softened
1 cup flour
¼ cup powdered sugar
2 tablespoons lemon juice
1 grated lemon rind
2 eggs beaten
1 cup sugar
2 tablespoons flour
½ teaspoon baking powder
Icing: mix 2 teaspoons lemon juice and ⅓ cup powdered sugar together

Preheat oven to 350 degrees F. In large bowl mix together butter, flour, and powdered sugar. Pat into bottom of 8-inch square pan. Bake 15 minutes. Sift together sugar, 2 tablespoons flour, and baking powder. Add eggs, lemon juice, and lemon rind. Spoon onto baked crust and bake 25 minutes more. When cool, frost with icing. Serves 6 to 8.

LEMON MERINGUE DESSERT

4 egg whites
½ teaspoon cream of tartar
⅛ teaspoon salt
1 grated lemon rind
¼ cup crushed pineapple
1 ½ teaspoon vanilla extract
1 cup sugar
4 egg yolks
½ cup sugar
2 tablespoons lemon juice

Preheat oven to 250 degrees F. In large bowl beat egg whites til very stiff. Add cream of tartar, salt, 1 cup sugar, and vanilla extract. Put into 13 x 9-inch pan and bake 1 hour. Combine other ingredients in double boiler and cook til thick. Cool and spread over meringue. Top with ¾ cup whipped cream, 2 tablespoons sugar, and 1 teaspoon vanilla extract. Sprinkle with coconut. Refrigerate 24 hours. Serves 6 to 8.

Lemon Mousse

10 egg whites
2 cups sugar
1 cup lemon juice
2 lemon rinds
Salt to taste
½ cup water
2 cups heavy cream

In large bowl whisk egg whites and sugar into a chiffon consistency. In a separate bowl combine the remaining ingredients til well-mixed. Gently fold together, and chill for 2 hours. Serve in glasses. Garnish with whipped cream and chocolate shavings. Serves 6 to 8.

Macadamia Fudge Torte

Filling

⅓ cup low-fat sweetened condensed milk
½ cup chocolate chips

Cake

1 package devil's food cake mix, pudding included
1 ½ teaspoon cinnamon
⅓ cup oil
16 ounces pears in light syrup, drained
2 eggs
⅓ cup macadamia nuts
1 teaspoon water

Sauce

16 ounces butterscotch, caramel, or fudge topping
⅓ cup milk

Preheat oven to 350 degrees F. Spray 10-inch spring form pan with nonstick spray. In small saucepan combine filling ingredients. Cook over medium heat til chocolate is melted, stirring occasionally.

In large bowl combine cake mix, cinnamon, and oil. Blend at low speed for 20 to 30 seconds til crumbly. Place pears in blender and blend til smooth.

In large bowl combine 2 ½ cups of the cake mixture, pears, and eggs. Beat at low speed til moistened. Beat for an additional 2 minutes at medium speed.

Spread batter evenly in spring form pan. Drop filling by spoonfuls over batter. Stir nuts and water into remaining cake mix. Sprinkle over filling and bake at 350 degrees F for 40 to 50 minutes or til top springs back when lightly touched in center. Cool 10 minutes. Remove sides of pan and cool an additional 90 minutes.

In small saucepan combine sauce ingredients and cook over low heat for 3 to 4 minutes or til well-blended. To serve spoon 2 tablespoons warm sauce onto each plate and then top with torte. Serves 12 to 15.

Margarita Marinated Strawberries

½ cup sugar
3 tablespoons lime juice
2 tablespoons triple sec
2 tablespoons tequila
3 pints strawberries

Mix sugar, lime juice, triple sec, and tequila together in medium bowl. Process 1 cup strawberries til smooth. Cut remaining strawberries in half. Combine purée and strawberries. Cover and refrigerate up to 8 hours before serving. Serves 12 to 15.

MINIATURE CREAM PUFFS

1 package small cream puff shells
8-ounce can crushed pineapple
1 cup whipped topping
3 ounces cream cheese

Slice tops off puffs and set aside. Mix cream cheese and whipped topping together at medium speed for 1 minute. Add slightly drained pineapple and mix again for 1 minute. Spoon mix into puffs and replace tops. Refrigerate til ready to serve.

Recipe from Stella D'oro® Anginetti Cookies

NEW NAPOLEONS

6 ounce package wonton-skin wrappers
2 tablespoons margarine, melted
4 teaspoons sugar
8 ounces whipped topping
1 pint strawberries

Preheat oven to 350 degrees F. Place 12 wonton wrappers in 1 layer on sheet of wax paper. With pastry brush, brush lightly with half the melted margarine and sprinkle with 1 teaspoon sugar.

Turn wontons over and brush lightly with rest of margarine and another teaspoon of sugar. Place wontons on large greased cookie sheet. Bake 10 to 12 minutes, turning over once til golden on both sides. Remove to wire rack to cool.

Repeat with remaining wrappers. If not used right away, store in tightly covered container. About 20 minutes before serving cut 4 small strawberries in half and reserve for garnish. Thinly slice remaining berries.

On each of 8 dessert plates place 1 baked wonton and spread 2 tablespoons whipped topping on each. Arrange half the sliced berries on whipped topping, and top with another wonton skin. Spread each with 2 tablespoons whipped topping and top with remaining sliced berries.

Place remaining 8 wontons on top. Spoon a dollop of whipped topping on each and garnish with halved berries. Serves 8.

OLD FASHIONED LEMON PUDDING CAKE

3 eggs, separated
1 cup sugar
¼ cup flour
¼ teaspoon salt
1 cup milk
¼ cup lemon juice

Preheat oven to 325 degrees F. In small bowl beat egg whites til stuff but not dry. Set aside. In medium bowl combine sugar, flour, and salt. In small bowl beat egg yolks and stir in milk and lemon juice.

Add wet mixture to flour mixture and mix well. Fold in egg whites and pour into 1-quart baking dish. Place dish in a larger pan, filled with 1 inch of water.

Bake 50 to 55 minutes or til top is well-browned. Cool about 30 minutes before serving. Place cake in a serving dish and spoon pudding over cake. Refrigerate any leftovers. Serves 6 to 8.

Orange Rum Poached Pineapple with Yogurt

1 fresh, ripe pineapple skinned with blemishes removed (pineapple is ripe if a leaf on top comes out easily when yanked)
1 cup orange juice, preferably fresh
2 tablespoons lemon juice, preferably fresh
1 cup packed brown sugar
¼ teaspoon vanilla extract
¼ cup dark rum
½ cup low-fat vanilla yogurt
2 tablespoons coconut liquor
2 tablespoons shredded coconut

Preheat oven to 250 degrees F. Spread coconut thinly on a cookie sheet and bake for about 5 to 10 minutes, til golden brown. Cut pineapple into ¾-inch rings, 8 slices per pineapple. In large nonstick skillet combine orange juice, lemon juice, brown sugar, and vanilla extract. Place over medium heat and bring to a boil. When sugar is dissolved, add pineapple and cover. Cook 1 minute and then reduce heat to low. Continue to cook for 4 minutes.

Remove pan from heat and add rum. Return to heat and cook for 30 seconds. Using a slotted spoon remove pineapple from pan and place in large bowl. Place pan over medium heat and cook til liquid is reduced and somewhat thick, 5 to 7 minutes. Pour syrup over pineapple and refrigerate for 2 hours. Add coconut liquor to yogurt and mix well. Serve pineapple with yogurt drizzled on top and sprinkled with toasted coconut. Serves 6 to 8.

Panic

1 white cake mix
2 cans cherry pie filling
½ cup pecans
½ cup shredded coconut
1 stick butter, melted

Preheat oven to 350 degrees F. Place pie filling in bottom of 13 x 9-inch pan and pour cake mix over filling. Do not stir. Add coconut, pecans, and butter in chunks.

Bake for 30 minutes. Serves 8.

Peach Delight

1 box vanilla wafers, crushed
⅓ pound margarine
1 cup powdered sugar
2 eggs
1 ½ large cans sliced peaches
1 pint whipped cream

Put ½ of the wafers in 13 x 9-inch pan. In large bowl beat eggs, margarine, and sugar til fluffy. Spread over crumbs; add drained peaches, then cream, and then crumbs.

Chill before serving. Serves 8 to 10.

Peanut Butter Banana Crunch

6 bananas, sliced
1 tablespoon lemon juice
½ teaspoon cinnamon
½ cup flour
½ cup packed brown sugar
⅓ cup chunky peanut butter
3 tablespoons margarine

Preheat oven to 375 degrees F. Place banana slices in 8-inch round baking dish. Add lemon juice and cinnamon, stirring lightly to cover bananas. In small bowl combine flour and brown sugar. Cut in peanut butter and margarine til mixture is crumbly. Sprinkle over bananas.

Bake for 25 minutes. Serve with whipped cream, if desired. Serves 6 to 8.

Pineapple Dessert

1 package yellow cake mix
1 small package vanilla pudding
8 ounces cream cheese, softened

Make cake as directed in 10 ½ x 8-inch pan. Make pudding as directed. Add cream cheese to pudding and beat til smooth. Spread over cake. Drain and add 1 can crushed pineapple.

Top with whipped topping and chopped nuts. Serves 6 to 8.

Raspberry Delight

1 package raspberry gelatin
1 cup hot water
1 can red raspberries, drained
1 box frozen raspberries
¾ cup chopped pecans
Vanilla wafers
1 cup whipped cream
⅛ pound small marshmallows

In large bowl dissolve gelatin in hot water and add drained raspberries. Whip til mix is slightly thickened.

Add whipped cream and partially thawed frozen berries. Add marshmallows and chopped nuts. Arrange vanilla wafers on bottom and sides of flat glass dish.

Add above mixture, alternating layers with vanilla wafers, til dish is filled.

Serve with whipped cream, if desired. This dish should be prepared the day before serving. Serves 10.

Raspberry Ice Cream Pie

1 package raspberry gelatin
1 ⅔ cup hot water
1 tablespoon lemon juice
1 pint vanilla ice cream
1 cup fresh raspberries
1 meringue shell, 9 to 10 inches

In large bowl dissolve gelatin in hot water. Add lemon juice and chill til partially set.

Beat in ice cream. Fold in raspberries and turn into meringue shell. Chill til firm, about 1 hour. Garnish with whole raspberries. Serves 12.

Strawberry Dessert Nachos

3 cups sliced strawberries
⅓ cup sugar
¼ cup amaretto
½ cup low-fat sour cream
½ cup whipped topping
2 tablespoons sugar
1 teaspoon cinnamon
6 to 7 flour tortillas
Butter flavored cooking spray
2 teaspoons cinnamon-sugar mix
2 tablespoons toasted sliced almonds
2 teaspoons semisweet chocolate

Combine strawberries, ⅓ cup sugar, and amaretto in a large container. Cover and chill for 30 minutes. Drain and save juice for other uses.

In a separate container combine sour cream, whipped topping, and 2 tablespoons cinnamon. Cover and chill. Preheat oven to 400 degrees F.

Cut tortillas into 8 wedges and arrange on 2 cookie sheets lightly coated with spray. Sprinkle with cinnamon-sugar.

Bake about 7 minutes or til crisp. Place wedges on plate and top with strawberry-sour cream mix. Garnish with almonds and chocolate chips. Serves 6 to 8.

Strawberry Meringue Pie

3 egg whites
1 cup sugar
1 teaspoon vanilla extract
1 ¼ teaspoon baking powder
¾ cup chopped nuts
14 crushed butter crackers
1 package frozen strawberries
1 cup whipping cream, whipped

Preheat oven to 325 degrees F. In a medium bowl beat egg whites til stiff. Add sugar and vanilla extract. In a large bowl mix together baking powder, butter crackers, and nuts.

Fold in egg white mixture. Bake in a well-greased 9-inch pan for 45 minutes. Cool thoroughly.

Whip cream and fold in strawberries. Fill shell with whipped cream and berry mixture. Chill 1 hour before serving. Serves 6.

Upside-down Raisin Pudding

1 tablespoon butter, softened
½ cup packed brown sugar
½ cup milk
½ cup raisins
1 cup flour
2 teaspoons baking powder
Pinch of salt

Preheat oven to 375 degrees F. Combine ingredients in a large bowl and spoon batter into a greased 13 x 9-inch pan.

In a large bowl mix 2 cups boiling water, 1 cup packed brown sugar, and 1 tablespoon butter. Pour over the above batter. Bake for 30 minutes. Serves 8.

Vanilla Cream Mold with Caramel Sauce

3 packages unflavored gelatin
1 cup sugar
¾ teaspoon salt
4 cups milk
4 teaspoons vanilla extract
8 ounces flaked coconut
4 cups heavy cream
¼ cup margarine
¼ cup flour
3 cups half-and-half
1 ½ cups packed brown sugar

No less than 5 hours before serving, mix gelatin, sugar, and salt in a 2-quart pan. Gradually add milk.

Cook over medium heat, stirring til gelatin is completely dissolved. Remove from heat and add vanilla extract.

Refrigerate til mixture mounds slightly when dropped from spoon, about 1 hour. Preheat oven to 350 degrees F. On a lightly greased cookie sheet spread coconut and toast in oven for 25 to 30 minutes. Stir to brown evenly. Cool and store.

In large bowl whip cream to form soft peaks and fold in gelatin mixture. Pour into 12 cup ring mold, refrigerate til set, about 3 hours.

In a 2-quart saucepan, over medium heat, melt margarine. Remove from heat and add flour til blended.

Gradually stir in half-and-half, add brown sugar and ¾ teaspoon salt. Stir constantly til mix is thick, cover and refrigerate.

To serve reheat sauce til warm, un-mold ring, and pour sauce and sprinkle toasted coconut on each serving. Serves 14.

Yum-yum Dessert

60 butter crackers, crushed
1 stick margarine, melted
2 packages instant chocolate pudding mix
½ gallon vanilla ice cream
Whipped topping

Combine crushed crackers and margarine til crumbly. Press ⅔ of this mixture into a 13 x 9-inch pan. In large mixing bowl mix 2 packages of instant chocolate pudding with 1 ½ cups of milk. Do not beat.

Fold in ½ gallon of vanilla ice cream and place ⅓ of crackers on top. Top with whipped topping. Serves 8 to 10.

Warm-up Dishes

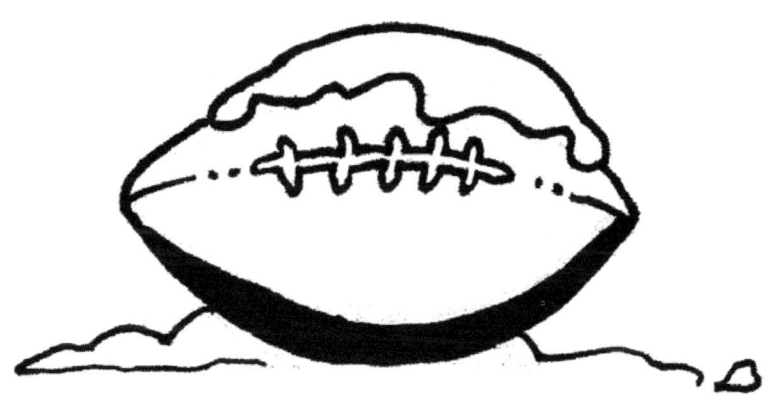

SNOWSTORM SOUPS

The Snow Bowl Game ◇ Let it Snow

Although we both graduated from high school in 1945, because of my brief Navy service during the final year of World War II, I was a year later starting to college than was Dittie. In addition, at Ohio State University the Engineering curriculum was five years long rather than the traditional four years. Thus, Dittie graduated as an Occupational Therapist in 1949, and in the autumn of 1950 I was just starting my final year at OSU.

Dittie's parents would not let us get married until after I graduated, so we were apart most of the time. It was with special anticipation that I looked forward to Thanksgiving that year. Dittie was to spend the holiday with her family in Connersville, Indiana, and myself with my family in Lima, Ohio, but Dittie's parents were to drop her off at OSU for the weekend and then she would go home to Cleveland by bus on Monday.

We both arrived in Columbus on Friday, as scheduled. Mom and Dad had tickets and were planning to stay overnight and then go to the Ohio State versus Michigan football game on Saturday. It had started to snow, however, and the forecast was for flurries overnight and into Saturday, so my parents decided to give up their tickets and go home rather than get caught in game-day traffic with snow on the road.

The flurries continued through the night and by morning the snow was several inches deep. The flurries still continued with the forecast of heavier snowfall still to come. Undaunted by the several inches on the ground and the continued reinforcements falling from the heavy clouds overhead, about noon our group joined many others headed for the stadium. This was, after all, THE game of the year. The rivalry between the two schools was (and still is today) so strong that to both teams winning or losing this game was tantamount to winning or losing their entire season.

Our seats were up in C-Deck, at the top of the stadium. Normally they were ideal seats for watching the game, but that day they were cold and piled with snow. There we stayed, nonetheless, caught up in the spirit of the game. There were some other spirits around if you were so inclined. The steps leading up to the higher seats were covered with snow, of course, and with the traffic of people walking over them the snow was packed pretty hard and was slippery. At one point during the game, we heard a voice behind us say, "Somebody grab the bottle!" We looked back and there came a man sliding down the snow slide that used to be a stairway, holding a bottle high with one hand, and trying to grab a bleacher seat with the other. Quick as a flash, Dittie held out her hand and grabbed the bottle as he went sliding by. Fortunately he was able to stop himself before going over the edge and onto the seats (and people) far below in A-Deck. He did manage to make his way back up to where we sat and retrieve his bottle.

The game was only a series of sliding attempts at running, punts, fumbles, and field goal attempts. Michigan won the game, but we had fun anyway. The game later was dubbed the Snow Bowl Game of 1950.

After the game, we returned to Neil Hall dorm where Dittie was staying with friends who still lived there. People straggled in wet, cold, tired, and hungry for an hour or more after the game. I am sure that some looked upon that storm as a curse, but for Dittie and me it was a blessing. The highways were impassable for about three days with no bus traffic possible. Thus, Dittie was unable to leave for home until Wednesday. We spent the extra days with our friends having snowball fights, building snowmen, pushing cars out of snowdrifts, and all those fun things you do when you are young and with the people you love most but who are not parents or family.

I have no idea what we might have eaten later that evening, but in retrospect it sounds like it would have been an ideal time for some hot soup or chili.

CHILI

There are probably thousands of different ways people prepare chili, but I can only present one I find easy to prepare and I like.

3 strips bacon
1 pound ground beef (70% to 80% lean)
1 small onion, coarsely chopped
2 (15-ounce) cans diced tomatoes
15-ounce can red (or dark red) kidney beans
1 teaspoon chili powder*
1 tablespoon salt*

Cut bacon slices into approximately ¼-inch pieces. Cook the bacon in a 2-quart pan til crisp.

Add ground beef and onion and heat on medium-low til meat is cooked through, stirring enough to keep it from sticking to the pan.

Add tomatoes, beans, and seasonings. Bring to a boil, and then turn heat down to low and simmer for at least 2 hours. Stir occasionally, in case it begins to stick.

Top with crushed red pepper before serving. Serve with saltine crackers and apple sauce on the side.

*Adjust amounts to suit your own taste. This is the way I like it.

COOL SALSA

2 large tomatoes, skinned
½ small onion
1 clove garlic
1 teaspoon lime juice
1 teaspoon tequila
1 teaspoon white vinegar

Combine all ingredients in a food processor and pulse til you achieve the texture you want.

CRISPIER FRIES

In a large skillet heat cooking oil to high and add fry-cut potatoes. Cook on all sides til almost done, slightly browned on the edges and tender when poked with a fork.

Remove potatoes and let them cool for about 2 minutes. Return fries to the hot oil and cook the rest of the way.

Much crispier than regular fries!

Great Garlic Bread

1 loaf sliced bread
¼ cup butter
1 tablespoon olive oil
5 garlic cloves, minced
¼ cup fresh parsley, chopped

Preheat oven to 375 degrees F. Combine ingredients in a medium saucepan and bring to a boil for 1 minute. Spread on the bread slices.

Bake for 10 minutes and then broil on high til crispy, about 10 more minutes.

It is easier to spread chilled butter on the bread. After butter has chilled whip the mixture in a blender and then spread on slices.

Great Lamb Rub

1 head of garlic, peeled and chopped (use food processor, if available)
1 tablespoon fresh rosemary, chopped
1 tablespoon fresh parsley, chopped
1 tablespoon fresh thyme, chopped
½ teaspoon black pepper
1 tablespoon olive oil
¼ teaspoon cayenne pepper

Fresh spices are best, but dried ones will work too. If using dried spices use about ¼ of the quantities listed. Combine all ingredients in a food processor. Chop for about 10 to 20 seconds. Rub onto all sides of lamb.

Grill lamb to preferred level. Serve with rice pilaf.

Hearty Turkey Vegetable Soup

Turkey carcass
½ pound medium pearled barley
12-ounce package frozen chopped onion
20-ounce package frozen carrots
4 cans condensed green pea soup
2 tablespoons salt
Pepper to taste

Place broken up turkey carcass in 8-quart pot. Fill with water to approximately 4 inches from top. Bring to a boil.

Reduce heat, cover, and simmer til turkey bits fall easily from the bones. Remove bones from the broth. Separate any meat from the bones and return meat to the pot. Discard bones.

Return meat stock to heat. Add barley, salt, and pepper. Simmer for 30 minutes, stirring occasionally so barley does not stick. Add onions and carrots and continue simmering til barley and vegetables are tender.

Mix in 1 can of pea soup at a time with some of the broth. Add soup to the pot and continue simmering and stirring occasionally for 30 minutes.

Serve with crackers, croutons, French bread, or Italian Bread.

Italian Chicken Soup

2 tablespoons olive oil
1 cup onion, chopped
1 cup celery, chopped
2 cups fresh carrots, sliced
1 fresh or frozen chicken breast
10-ounce package Italian green beans, frozen
15-ounce can diced tomatoes
3 teaspoons chicken bouillon
8 ounces ricotta cavatelli, frozen
15-ounce can cannelloni beans
¼ teaspoon black pepper
½ teaspoon marjoram
¾ teaspoon basil

Sauté onion and celery in olive oil for about 5 minutes. Add 6 cups water, carrots, tomatoes, and bouillon. Bring to a boil, lower heat, and simmer for 10 minutes.

Add chicken breast. Simmer about 10 minutes. Add cavatelli, cannelloni beans, green beans, and herbs.

Continue to simmer til chicken is no longer pink, about 5 minutes.

Remove chicken breast and allow to cool. When chicken is cool enough to handle, cut into bite-size pieces. Return to pot and simmer til vegetables and cavatelli are tender, about 10 minutes. Serves 8.

Italian Spinach

1 package fresh spinach
¼ cup grated Parmesan cheese

Cook spinach in a large saucepan with ⅛ cup water til leaves are wilted. Spread spinach on a baking sheet and sprinkle with Parmesan cheese.

Place under broiler til cheese is crispy, about 3 minutes. Serves 2.

Lentil Soup

4 stalks celery, diced
1 large onion, diced
6 garlic cloves, minced
5 carrots, diced
1 green pepper, diced
1-pound bag lentils, washed and sorted
¼ cup regular rice
4 vegetable bouillon cubes
28-ounce can diced tomatoes
16-ounce can tomato sauce
1 tablespoon vegetable oil
3 ½ quarts water

In a large kettle sauté garlic, onion, pepper, and celery in oil for about 3 minutes til softened. Add water and bring to a boil.

Add lentils and carrots. Bring to a boil again and simmer about 10 minutes. Add rice and bring to a simmer again. Add tomatoes, tomato sauce, and vegetable bouillon cubes. Simmer on low for about 1 hour til lentils and rice are done and flavors are blended.

Mediterranean Eggplant Stew

2 tablespoons olive oil
1 medium onion, chopped
1 medium eggplant, diced
1 red bell pepper, seeded and diced
3 garlic cloves, minced
2 cups vegetable broth
1 ½ cups water
2 (14 ½-ounce) cans diced tomatoes
15-ounce can chickpeas, rinsed and drained
1 teaspoon paprika
1 teaspoon dried parsley
1 ½ teaspoons dried oregano
¼ teaspoon black pepper
1 tablespoon sugar
½ teaspoon salt

In a large saucepan heat oil and add onion. Cook for 8 to 10 minutes til soft.

Add eggplant and red bell pepper and cook for about 8 more minutes while stirring frequently.

Add garlic, paprika, parsley, and oregano and continue cooking for a few more minutes. Stir in broth, water, tomatoes, chickpeas, and sugar.

Bring to a boil, turn heat down, and simmer for about 30 minutes. Add salt and pepper. Serves 6.

Mexican Corn & Tortilla Soup

1 tablespoon canola oil
1 onion, diced
1 zucchini, diced
1 red bell pepper, seeded and diced
3 cloves garlic, minced
1 or 2 jalapeno peppers, seeded and diced
6 cups vegetable broth
14-ounce can diced tomatoes with juice
2 teaspoons oregano
2 teaspoons cumin
1 ½ cup corn kernels, fresh or frozen
4 (6-inch) flour tortillas cut into ½-inch wide strips

Heat oil in a large pot. Add onion and sauté for a couple of minutes. Add zucchini, red pepper, chili pepper, and garlic. Sauté for about 5 minutes.

Add broth, tomatoes, and seasonings. Bring to a boil and simmer for about 15 minutes.

Add corn and simmer for another 10 minutes or so. Add the tortilla strips during the last 5 minutes of cooking. Serves 8.

MULLIGATAWNY SOUP

1 tablespoon vegetable oil
½ cup onions, chopped
2 ribs celery, diced
1 large tart apple; peeled, cored, and chopped
1 sweet potato; peeled and finely chopped
2 tablespoons flour
½ teaspoon curry powder
4 cups reduced sodium vegetable or chicken broth
16-ounce can chunky tomatoes; with juice
1 teaspoon lemon juice
1 ½ teaspoons dried parsley
½ teaspoon pepper
1 cup skim or 1% milk

In a large stockpot sauté onion and celery in oil til tender, about 8 to 10 minutes.

Stir in apple, sweet potato, parsley, and curry. Cook, stirring occasionally, for 5 minutes or til vegetables are tender-crisp.

Sprinkle flour over mixture and stir well to blend. Add broth, tomatoes, and lemon juice.

Bring to a boil. Reduce heat, and simmer 15 to 20 minutes til all vegetables are tender. Add milk and black pepper. Stir well and serve. Serves 4.

MUSHROOM BARLEY SOUP

2 tablespoons olive oil
1 large onion, chopped
2 carrots, peeled and diced
2 ribs celery, diced
2 tablespoons flour
4 cloves garlic, minced
1 teaspoon thyme
6 cups vegetable broth
½ cup pearl barley
1 ½ pound fresh mushrooms; rinsed, dried, and sliced
1 tablespoon dried dill
1 tablespoon lemon juice
Black pepper to taste

Heat 1 tablespoon oil in a heavy soup pot and sauté onion, carrots, and celery til softened, but not brown, about 5 minutes. Add flour, garlic, and thyme and stir for a minute. Add 1 cup of broth and bring to a simmer, stirring constantly.

Add remaining broth and barley. Increase heat and bring to a simmer again. Reduce heat to low, cover, and simmer til barley is almost tender, about 35 minutes. Meanwhile, heat remaining tablespoon oil in a large skillet.

Add mushrooms and cook, stirring occasionally, til browned and tender, about 6 minutes. After barley has simmered for 35 minutes, add sautéed mushrooms and liquid to soup.

Simmer uncovered til barley is tender and flavors have blended, about 5 minutes longer. Stir in dill, lemon juice, and pepper. Serves 6.

New England Clam Chowder

1 tablespoon canola oil
1 medium onion, diced
2 carrots, diced
2 stalks celery, diced
2 medium potatoes, peeled and diced
3 (6 ½-ounce) cans chopped clams
2 ½ cups 1% milk
2 cups non-fat half-and-half
2 tablespoons cornstarch
¼ teaspoon garlic powder
¼ teaspoon thyme leaves

Sauté onion, carrot, and celery in canola oil for 5 to 7 minutes. Add potatoes and clams (with liquid) and simmer 6 to 8 minutes. Stir in 2 cups low-fat milk, half-and-half, garlic powder, and thyme leaves. Add cornstarch to remaining ½ cup milk, stirring til dissolved, and then add to soup. Heat til warmed, but do not boil. Serves 6.

Rice Pilaf

12 ounces chicken broth
1 cup rice
1 teaspoon fresh thyme, chopped
¼ small onion, diced
1 small tomato, diced
1 teaspoon fresh rosemary, chopped
1 carrot, diced
1 tablespoon fresh parsley, chopped
1 celery stalk; diced, with bit of leaves
1 tablespoon butter
1 teaspoon olive oil
4 cloves garlic, minced
Salt and pepper to taste

Heat butter and oil in a large skillet. When melted add rice, tomato, onion, celery, carrot, and garlic. Sauté for 1 minute. Add chicken broth and cook til rice is done, about 15 minutes. Serves 4.

Spicy Red Lentil Soup

1 tablespoon olive oil
2 onions, diced
6 cups vegetable broth
2 carrots, diced
2 stalks celery, diced
½ cup brown rice
1 cup red lentils
1 bay leaf
1 tablespoon fresh parsley, chopped
1 teaspoon ground coriander
2 teaspoons garam marsala
Salt and pepper to taste
Cilantro for garnish, optional

Heat oil in a large pot. Cook onion til soft. Add carrots and celery and cook a few more minutes. Add broth and bring to a boil. Add brown rice and simmer 10 to 15 minutes. Add herbs, spices, and lentils. Bring to a boil and simmer til rice is tender, about 30 minutes. Discard bay leaf. Garnish with cilantro, if desired. Serves 8.

Ultimate Meat Sauce

½ pound ground beef
½ pound spicy Italian sausage
1 can of your favorite tomato sauce
1 tablespoon olive oil
1 medium onion, chopped
8 cloves garlic, minced
⅛ cup chopped fresh parsley
⅛ cup chopped fresh basil

In a large skillet, combine oil, onion, and garlic. Sauté for about 1 minute. Add meat and stir til meat is cooked through. Strain off grease and add tomato sauce. Add basil and parsley. Cover and let simmer for at least 10 minutes.

July 21, 1951

This is the most important date in my life and I can't quite remember what happened during most of the day. I do remember that my parents, brother, sister, and I had stayed with Mr. and Mrs. Dalquist, friends of Dittie's parents, the night before. I also remember that my brother took me to a Cleveland Indians baseball game at Cleveland's Lakefront Stadium that afternoon. Dittie always maintained that it was a double-header, but I don't remember that—I don't even remember who won and I was, and still am, an Indians fan.

I do remember, though, that there was a wedding scheduled for 7:30—my wedding. I also remember seeing Dittie walking toward me down the church aisle, holding on to her Father's arm as if he might either get away, or as if she might fall if he was not holding her up. It was the most beautiful sight I have ever seen. Her hand trembled as it took mine; well, maybe it was my hand that was shaking. I guess we got through our vows though, because I remember kissing her in front of all those people and walking back up the aisle. This time Dittie was holding my arm.

Our reception was held in the ballroom of the Lake Shore Hotel in Lakewood. I had never waltzed before, but Dittie guided me through our first dance. Then she danced with her Father, I danced with my Mother, and when everyone else joined in the party really began. In fact, the party was so great that Dittie's father had to remind us we still had to drive to the Painesville Inn that night, and it was time to change into our travel clothes and get going.

When we got up the following morning it was raining, and I tried to spot our car from the window so we could dash right to it. I could not find it! There was a car that looked like ours, but it had an out-of-state license plate. I finally went out for a closer look and discovered it was our car! Our friends had put last year's plates on it (they were a different color); evidently hoping we would be stopped by the Highway Patrol. The real plates were in the trunk and we had no further problems, expect for trying to stay dry. I will leave the rest of our one-week honeymoon to your imagination. Let me just say that a new life began for me on July 21, 1951.

Special Dinners

OUR FIRST THANKSGIVING

A Little Dressed Up ◊ Celebration Dinners

Dittie and I were married in July, and it was now November with Thanksgiving approaching. Dittie's parents had gone to her Grandmother's house in Indiana for the holiday, leaving the two of us to celebrate. This was too small a crowd to warrant a turkey, so Dittie decided we would have roast duck instead. She went shopping for the duck, sweet potatoes, dressing, and something for dessert, but I forget what. I am only now beginning to appreciate the courage of my new bride in planning and preparing such a fancy dinner.

To make the occasion extra special, we drove to her parents' house where our wedding presents were being stored since we did not have any extra room in our apartment. We picked up two settings of our new china, sterling silver, and crystal. We also picked up the necessary serving dishes and the sterling silver meat platter, which was sufficient for a large turkey. Her first big dinner was beautifully done and smelled delicious. Then, to my surprise, she handed me the carving knife and fork. I had never before carved anything more complicated than a steak while in the process of eating it, and now I was expected to carve a duck?

Well, if Dittie could prepare a whole roast duck dinner, carving the duck certainly could not be too difficult, right? Wrong! Ducks have fat on them, and when you cook them the slippery grease winds up on the outside of the duck. True, I had the carving fork to hold it with, but that duck would not remain stationary on the platter. I wound up chasing that darned bird from one end of the platter to the other, over and over. The silver tray still carries the battle scars of our first Thanksgiving dinner.

If you are planning a special meal for family, friends, or even for yourself, you might try selecting your courses from the following menu items:

ENTRÉES

APRICOT GLAZED PORK TENDERLOIN

1 pound pork tenderloin
1 tablespoon olive oil, divided
2 medium carrots, diced
1 small onion, diced
½ small red pepper, diced
1 cup instant rice, uncooked
1 cup chicken broth
10-ounce jar apricot spread

Preheat oven to 425 degrees F. Pat pork dry and season with salt and pepper. In large skillet over medium heat, brown pork thoroughly on all sides in 1 tablespoon of oil. Remove from skillet and set aside. Add carrots, onions, and red pepper to skillet and sauté til onions start to soften, about 2 minutes.

Add rice and stir to coat with oil. Add chicken broth, salt, and pepper. Bring mixture to a boil. Place rice mixture in 13 x 9-inch baking dish and place pork on top of rice. Spoon apricot spread over pork and cover with foil. Bake for 20 minutes. Remove foil and bake for 5 more minutes. Serves 3 or 4.

CLAY POT CHICKEN

1 whole 2 to 3 pound chicken (check cavity for giblets and rinse entire chicken with water)
1 cup chicken broth
3 to 4 potatoes
1 medium onion
5 stalks celery with leaves
6 (or more) carrots
5 garlic cloves, peeled
1 to 2 tablespoons olive oil
1 teaspoon fresh thyme
⅛ teaspoon cayenne pepper
Salt and pepper to taste
¼ cup white wine, optional

Soak clay pot and lid in water for 15 minutes. Cut onion into slices and cut celery into sticks and place in a layer in the bottom of the pot.

Place chicken on top of onions and celery. Peel carrots and cut them in half. Peel potatoes and cut them in quarters. Place potatoes and carrots around the chicken along with garlic.

Drizzle oil over chicken and vegetables. Pour broth and wine into the pot. Sprinkle cayenne, thyme, salt, and pepper on the chicken and vegetables. Place lid on pot and put in cold oven (pot will crack if placed in hot oven). Turn oven on and heat to 450 degrees F and cook for 85 minutes. Serves 4.

COQ AU VÎN

¼ cup butter
¼ cup salad oil
2 frying chickens, cut up
1 teaspoon salt
¼ cup flour
⅔ cup burgundy
½ cup chicken broth
½ pound fresh sliced mushrooms
4 medium onions, quartered
2 tablespoons chopped parsley
Dash of thyme, marjoram, salt, and pepper to taste

Preheat oven to 350 degrees F. In large skillet heat butter and oil. Brown chicken pieces on all sides and transfer to a 2-quart casserole dish. Add flour to drippings in skillet and blend. Add wine and broth. Cook and stir til mixture boils and thickens. Add remaining ingredients and pour over chicken. Cover and bake for about 1 hour. Add more wine, if needed, to thin sauce to desired consistency. Serves 8.

Ryan's Beef Brisket (Simplified)

1 convenient size beef brisket
2 shallots, chopped
4 cloves garlic, chopped
12 ounces beef broth
Salt and pepper

Preheat oven to 250 degrees F. In a foil bag cover brisket with shallots and garlic. Add salt, pepper, and broth to bag. Seal completely. Bake in oven for at least 6 hours. The longer it cooks, the more tender the meat gets.

Tiffin Style Beef Stroganoff

1 ½-pound beef filet
2 tablespoons finely chopped onion
½ pound sliced fresh mushrooms
1 tablespoon flour
2 cups sour cream
1 teaspoon tomato paste
1 ½ teaspoons Worcestershire sauce
3 finely sliced sweet pickles
½ teaspoon nutmeg
Salt, pepper, paprika, and butter to taste

Cut filet of choice beef into julienne strips 1-inch long and 1 ¼-inch wide. Season with salt, pepper, and paprika. Heat butter the size of an egg in a large skillet and sauté beef quickly on high til just medium-rare. Remove meat from pan.

In same pan sauté onion and cook til about half done. Add sliced fresh mushrooms and cook a few more minutes, adding butter if needed.

Sprinkle flour over the mushrooms. Stir as you slowly add sour cream. To this sauté add tomato paste, Worcestershire, pickles, ¼ teaspoon salt, and nutmeg.

Return meat to sauce. Serve meat over cooked rice. Serves 4 to 6.

Side Dishes

Broccoli Puffs

10-ounce package frozen broccoli
1 cup mushroom soup
¼ cup mayonnaise
¼ cup milk
1 egg, beaten
2 to 3 ounces shredded sharp cheese

Preheat oven to 350 degrees F. Combine ingredients in a large bowl and spoon into a 13 x 9-inch baking pan. Top with ¼ cup bread crumbs mixed with 1 tablespoon melted margarine. Bake for 20 to 30 minutes, or til custard-like. Serves 6.

Cheese Potatoes

2 pounds frozen hash browns
¼ pound margarine, melted
2 cups sour cream
1 can celery soup
1 can cheddar cheese soup
1 medium onion, diced

Preheat oven to 350 degrees F. Combine ingredients in a large bowl and spoon into a 13 x 9-inch dish and top with crushed potato chips.

Bake for 30 to 35 minutes. Serves 6 to 8.

CRUNCHY CHEESE POTATOES

1 cup sour cream
½ cup milk
1 tablespoon minced chives
½ teaspoon salt
¼ teaspoon pepper
6 medium potatoes; peeled and sliced ¼-inch thick
1 cup shredded sharp cheddar cheese
½ cup finely crushed cornflakes
Additional chives, optional

Preheat oven to 350 degrees F. In large bowl combine sour cream, milk, chives, salt, and pepper. Add potatoes and mix thoroughly.

Spread in a 15 x 10-inch pan. Combine cheese and cornflakes, and sprinkle over potatoes.

Bake for 50 to 60 minutes or til tender. Sprinkle with additional chives, if desired. Serves 6 to 8.

GLAZED PEARL ONIONS

2 pounds pearl onions
3 tablespoons margarine
2 tablespoons currant jelly
2 teaspoons sugar
¼ teaspoon salt

In deep skillet over high heat, heat 1 inch of water to boiling. Add onions and heat to boiling. Boil for 1 minute and drain. Peel onions, leaving a little of root ends to help hold shape during cooking. In same skillet over high heat, heat 1 inch of water to boiling. Add onions, heat to boiling, reduce heat to low, and cover. Simmer for 5 to 10 minutes til onions are tender, drain.

Wipe skillet dry and over high heat cook onions, margarine, currant jelly, sugar, and salt. Cook, stirring occasionally, til onions are browned and glazed, about 10 minutes. Serves 8.

GRAND MARNIER SWEET POTATOES

1 tablespoon orange peel
2 cups mandarin oranges, reserve a few for garnish
¼ cup plus 1 to 2 tablespoons packed brown sugar
½ cup Grand Marnier
¼ cup cream
¼ cup melted butter
1 teaspoon salt
4 cups cooked sweet potatoes, mashed

Preheat oven to 350 degrees F. In a saucepan over low heat combine orange peel, ¼ cup brown sugar, Grand Marnier, cream, butter, and salt. Stir til combined and smooth, do not boil. In large bowl beat mixture into mashed potatoes, and fold in the mandarin orange segments. Put everything into a 13 x 9-inch casserole dish. Top with the reserved mandarin orange segments and additional brown sugar.

Bake uncovered for 35 to 40 minutes. Casserole may be made well in advance and refrigerated til ready to bake. Serves 4 to 6.

HONEY GLAZED CARROTS

10 to 12 small carrots
3 tablespoons butter
1 tablespoon packed brown sugar
2 tablespoons honey

Preheat oven to 350 degrees F. Cover carrots with water in small saucepan and cook over medium heat til carrots reach desired softness. Mix butter, honey, and brown sugar over medium-low heat in separate saucepan, stirring til mixture is liquefied and blended. On a baking sheet, coat carrots with glaze and place in oven for about 10 minutes, turning as needed to coat carrots.

ORIENTAL CASHEW ASPARAGUS

1 pound fresh asparagus; trimmed and bias cut into 1-inch pieces
1 ½ cups quartered fresh mushrooms
1 medium onion, sliced thin
¼ cup chopped red sweet pepper
2 tablespoons butter
1 teaspoon cornstarch
Pepper to taste
1 tablespoon teriyaki sauce
2 tablespoons cashew halves
2 tablespoons sherry

Steam asparagus over, but not touching, gently boiling water. Cover and reduce heat and steam for 2 minutes. Add mushrooms, onion, and red pepper. Cover and steam for 2 to 5 minutes more or til tender-crisp. Remove basket and discard liquid. In same saucepan melt margarine and stir in cornstarch and pepper. Add teriyaki sauce, sherry, and 2 teaspoons water. Cook and stir til thickened and bubbly. Return vegetables to pan and toss gently to coat. Top each serving with cashews. Serves 4 to 6.

ROASTED VIDALIA ONIONS

4 medium Vidalia onions; peeled and cut into 8 wedges
Olive oil flavored cooking spray
1 teaspoon dried thyme
½ teaspoon salt
¼ teaspoon pepper
1 tablespoon balsamic vinegar

Preheat oven to 350 degrees F. Place onions on jelly roll pan slightly coated with spray and lightly coat onions with spray. Sprinkle thyme, salt, and pepper over onions. Bake for 30 minutes. Turn onions and bake for 25 minutes longer. Place on serving dish and drizzle with vinegar. Serves 4 to 6.

SWEET POTATOES WITH PECAN TOPPING

2 large sweet potatoes; peeled and cut into 1-inch pieces
6 tablespoons unsalted butter
1 large egg
6 tablespoons sugar
1 teaspoon pumpkin pie spice
Salt

For **Pecan Topping** combine the following:

1 ½ cups crushed cornflakes
½ cup packed brown sugar
½ cup chopped pecans
6 tablespoons unsalted butter, melted

Preheat oven to 400 degrees F. Boil potatoes in large saucepan covered with water til tender, about 15 minutes. Drain and transfer potatoes to large bowl and add butter.

Use electric mixer and beat til smooth. Add egg, sugar, spice, and salt. Beat to blend and transfer mix to 8 x 8-inch dish.

Bake potatoes til they begin to brown around edges and become slightly puffed, about 25 minutes. Meanwhile, make topping and spoon over potatoes. Bake til golden brown and crisp, about 10 minutes longer. Serves 4 to 6.

WILD RICE

¼ pound butter
1 cup rice
½ cup slivered almonds
2 tablespoons chopped onion
2 tablespoons green pepper
2 small cans sliced mushrooms
¾ cup chicken broth, add more if dry

Preheat oven to 325 degrees F. Combine ingredients. Bake in covered 13 x 9-inch dish for 2 hours. Serves 4.

SALADS

APRICOT SALAD

1 large package apricot gelatin
20 ounces crushed pineapple, drained (save juice)
2 cups boiling water
1 cup small marshmallows
3 large bananas, mashed
2 scant cups cold water including all but ½ cup pineapple juice

In a large bowl dissolve gelatin into boiling water. Mix in marshmallows, pineapple, water, and bananas. Pour into pan, cover, and refrigerate overnight.

Topping

1 egg
2 tablespoons flour
½ cup sugar
½ cup pineapple juice
8 ounces whipped topping

In a medium saucepan combine ingredients and cook over medium heat til thickened. Remove from heat. Add 2 tablespoons of butter and 3 ounces of softened cream cheese. Cover lightly and refrigerate overnight.

The next day blend topping into container of whipped topping and spread over gelatin. Chill several hours and top with nuts. Serves 10 to 12.

BROCCOLI SALAD

2 bunches broccoli, chopped fine
1 pound bacon, cooked and crumbled
½ cup raisins
½ cup sunflower seeds

In a large bowl mix broccoli, raisins and seeds together. Add ½ cup mayonnaise, ½ cup or less of sugar, and 2 teaspoons vinegar. Crumble bacon on top and toss again. Refrigerate 3 hours or overnight. Serves 8 to 10.

CHRISTMAS GELATIN SALAD

In a large bowl combine 1 package strawberry gelatin in 1 cup boiling water. Add 1 package frozen cranberry relish and a dash of salt.

Spread mixture in 13 x 9-dish, or use gelatin molds. Chill til firm

14 ounces crushed pineapple
1 package lime gelatin
1 ¼ cups boiling water
2 cups small marshmallows
3 ounces cream cheese, softened
½ cup mayonnaise
½ cup whipped cream

Drain pineapple and reserve syrup. In a large bowl dissolve lime gelatin in boiling water. Add marshmallows and let them melt. Add pineapple syrup and chill til partially set.

Blend in cream cheese, mayonnaise, and pineapple into marshmallow mixture. If mix is too thin, chill a little. Fold in whipped cream. Pour over first mixture and chill.

This second mixture may be tinted a festive green, if desired. Serves 16 to 20.

EDIE'S SALAD

½ cup sliced almonds
3 tablespoons sugar
½ head iceberg lettuce
½ head romaine lettuce
3 green onion, finely chopped
11-ounce can mandarin oranges, drained

Dressing

½ teaspoon salt
Dash of pepper
¼ cup vegetable oil
Dash of hot sauce
2 tablespoons sugar
2 tablespoons vinegar

In small skillet over medium heat cook almonds and sugar, stirring constantly til almonds are coated and sugar is dissolved. Cool and store in airtight container. Mix dressing and chill. Mix lettuce and onions. Just before serving add almonds and oranges. Toss with dressing. Serves 10 to 12.

FROZEN BING CHERRY SALAD

2 cups sour cream
2 teaspoons lemon juice
½ cup sugar
1 banana, diced
8 ounces crushed pineapple, drained
Red food coloring
1 pound pitted sweet cherries, drained
1 cup chopped pecans

In a large bowl combine first 6 ingredients and lightly fold in nuts and cherries. Spoon into cupcake papers and freeze. Remove from freezer 15 minutes before serving. Serves 12.

FROZEN CRANBERRY SALAD

1 cup jellied cranberry sauce, broken up with a fork
8 ½ ounces crushed pineapple
1 cup marshmallows
1 tablespoon lemon juice
½ cup chopped nuts

In a large bowl mix all ingredients together. Spoon into a 13 x 9-inch pan, cover and freeze.

Topping

½ package non-dairy whipped topping
¼ cup mayonnaise
¼ cup powdered sugar

Mix topping ingredients and spread on top. Serves 8.

FROZEN PINEAPPLE SALAD

½ pint whipping cream, whipped
½ pint sour cream
1 tablespoon lemon juice
¾ cup sugar
½ teaspoon salt
9 ounces crushed pineapple, drained
⅓ cup maraschino cherries
¼ cup chopped nuts
2 medium bananas, chopped

In large bowl blend whipped cream and sour cream. Add lemon juice, sugar, and salt. Blend thoroughly.

Fold in pineapple gently. Add cherries, nuts, and bananas and mix lightly.

Spoon into muffin tins lined with cupcake papers. Freeze. Remove about 30 minutes before serving time. Serves 12.

Layered Orange Treat

2 packages orange or pineapple gelatin and 2 cups boiling water
1 pint orange sherbet
11 ounces mandarin oranges

In a large bowl dissolve 1 gelatin package in 1 cup water. Blend in sherbet and pour into 1 ½-quart mold. Freeze til firm. Dissolve remaining gelatin in remaining water. Drain oranges, measuring syrup, and add enough cold water to make 1 cup. Add this mixture to the orange gelatin. Pour over frozen layer, chill til firm, at least 30 minutes, and un-mold on lettuce. Serves 10 to 12.

Frozen layer may be made ahead and stored in freezer for a week. Add second layer at least 30 minutes before serving.

Oriental Salad

1 head lettuce, torn into small pieces
1 cup mandarin oranges (5 ounces), drained
Slivered almonds, toasted in bacon fat
French-fried onions
1 pound bacon

Dressing

2 ½ tablespoons vinegar
2 ½ tablespoons honey
½ tablespoon lemon juice
⅓ cup sugar

Combine dressing ingredients in a saucepan and gently heat til sugar dissolves. Cool, add ½ cup oil and shake well. Layer lettuce, oranges, almonds, and onions in salad bowl. Toss with dressing before serving. Serves 8.

24 Hour Salad

1 head lettuce
¼ cup chopped onion
1 cup finely chopped celery
6 ounces sliced water chestnuts
1 package frozen peas
1 ½ cup mayonnaise
2 tablespoons sugar
4 ounces grated cheddar cheese
¾ pound fried bacon, crumbled

Shred lettuce in 18 x 14-inch pan, sprinkle with onion, then celery, water chestnuts, and peas. Spread mayonnaise on like frosting. Sprinkle on sugar and cheese. Cover well and refrigerate overnight. Sprinkle with bacon before serving. Do not toss, instead cut into squares.

DESSERTS

BANANA FLAMBÉ AU GRAND MARNIER

4 firm bananas
Juice of 1 lemon
Flour
½ cup packed brown sugar
2 tablespoons chopped maraschino cherries
3 tablespoons Grand Marnier

Peel bananas and slice in half lengthwise. Brush with lemon juice and dust lightly with flour.

In large skillet over medium heat sauté bananas in hot butter, turning to lightly brown both sides. Sprinkle with brown sugar and scatter with cherries.

Pour Grand Marnier over bananas and ignite. Serve flaming. Serves 4.

BLACK FOREST CHERRY CAKE

2 cups flour
2 teaspoons baking powder
6 eggs
2 cups sugars
4 teaspoons lemon juice
¾ cup hot milk
Maraschino cherries
German sweet chocolate curls

Preheat oven to 350 degrees F. In a medium bowl sift together flour and baking powder. In a large bowl beat eggs til fluffy, about 10 minutes. Gradually add sugar to eggs, beating constantly. Add lemon juice. Fold in flour, a little at a time. Add hot milk, mixing quickly til batter is smooth. Lightly grease and flour three 9-inch round cake pans.

Divide batter between pans. Bake for 25 minutes, and test with toothpick. When cool, slice each layer into two thin layers.

Place first layer on serving plate. Spread with ½ chocolate filling (below). Add second layer and spread with a scant cup of kirsch crème (below). Add third layer and spread with remaining chocolate filling. Add fourth layer and spread with scant cup whipped cream. Top with fifth layer and spread cherry filling (below) over it. Add sixth layer and spread remaining kirsch crème over top and sides. Garnish with cherries and curls. Refrigerate at least 1 hour before serving. Serves 12 or more when thinly sliced.

Cherry Filling

1 can tart red cherries in heavy syrup
8 drops red food coloring

Cook together in a saucepan over medium heat, stirring constantly til thick and clear. Cool.

Chocolate Filling

1 bar German sweet chocolate
1 cup whipping cream, whipped

Melt chocolate over hot water, cool to room temperature. Fold in cream. Cool 20 minutes.

Kirsch Crème

2 cups whipping cream
Pinch of salt
3 tablespoons kirsch

Whip cream til stiff and add salt while you beat and then fold in kirsch.

Black Forest Crêpes

21-ounce can cherry pie filling, chilled
2 tablespoons cherry liqueur
¼ cup blanched almonds
⅔ cup milk
¼ cup flour
2 eggs
2 tablespoons butter, softened
3 ounces semisweet chocolate
1 cup whipping cream
¼ cup toasted slivered almonds

Mix pie filling and cherry liqueur, set aside. Place blanched almonds in blender, cover, and blend til fine.

Add milk, flour, eggs, and butter to blender. Cover and blend til smooth. Heat a small greased skillet and spoon in 2 tablespoons batter. Tilt skillet to spread batter. Brown on one side and invert crêpe over paper towel.

Repeat to make 12 crêpes. Melt chocolate over low heat and cool. Whip cream to soft peaks and fold in chocolate. Mixture will look speckled.

Spoon 2 tablespoons chocolate mixture down the center of un-browned side of each crêpe. Roll up.

Place 2 crêpes on a plate. Top with ⅓ cup cherry mixture, remaining chocolate mixture, and almonds. Serves 6.

Chocolate Mint Dessert

Cake Layer

1 cup flour
1 cup sugar
½ cup margarine, softened
4 eggs
1 ½ cups chocolate syrup

Preheat oven to 350 degrees F. Grease 13 x 9-inch pan. In large bowl combine flour, sugar, margarine, eggs, and chocolate syrup.

Beat til smooth. Pour into pan and bake for 25 to 30 minutes, or til top springs back when lightly touched.

Cool completely in pan. Spread Mint Cream Center (below) on cake, cover cake, and chill. Pour Chocolate Topping (below) over chilled dessert. Cover and chill for at least 1 hour before serving. Serves 12.

Mint Cream Center

2 cups powdered sugar
½ cup butter, softened
1 tablespoon water
½ to ¾ teaspoon mint extract
3 drops green food coloring

In small bowl combine all ingredients and beat til smooth.

Chocolate Topping

6 tablespoons butter
1 cup semisweet chocolate chips

In small saucepan over very low heat, melt butter and chocolate chips. Remove from heat and stir til smooth. Cool slightly.

Chocolate Torte Royale

2 egg whites
¼ teaspoon salt
½ teaspoon vinegar
½ cup sugar
¼ teaspoon cinnamon

Cover a cookie sheet with a piece of paper. Draw an 8-inch circle in center. In a large bowl beat egg whites, salt, and vinegar til soft peaks form.

Preheat oven to 275 degrees F. In a small bowl blend sugar and cinnamon together and gradually add to egg whites. Beat til very stiff peaks form and all the sugar has dissolved.

Spread within circle, making the bottom ½-inch thick and mounding around edge, making it 1 ¾-inch high.

For trim, form ridges on outside with back of teaspoon. Bake in very slow oven for 1 hour. Turn off heat and let dry in oven with door closed for about 2 hours. Peel off paper.

Twin Cream Fillings

1 cup chocolate chips
2 beaten egg yolks
¼ cup water
1 cup heavy cream
¼ cup sugar
¼ teaspoon cinnamon

In a small saucepan melt chocolate over hot, but not boiling, water. Cool slightly, and then spread 2 tablespoons of chocolate over bottom of cooled meringue shell.

To remaining chocolate blend in egg yolk and water. Chill til mixture is thick.

Combine cream, sugar, and cinnamon in a medium mixing bowl. Whip til stiff. Spread ½ over chocolate in shell and fold remainder into chocolate mixture. Spread on top.

Chill several hours or overnight. Trim with whipped cream and pecans. Serves 8 to 10.

Chocolate Trifle

Chocolate cake mix
6 tablespoons Kahlúa
Chocolate pudding mix (1 large or 2 small packages)
6 chocolate covered toffee bars, frozen
1 pint heavy cream, whipped

Bake the chocolate cake according to package directions in two 8-inch round pans. Put one layer in bottom of serving dish (approximately 8 ½ inches across and 5 to 6 inches deep).

Spread 3 tablespoons Kahlúa on top of layer in dish. Mix chocolate pudding as per package directions. Spread chocolate pudding on first layer.

Break up the 3 frozen chocolate covered toffee bars into bite-size pieces and distribute evenly on top of pudding layer.

Spread ½ pint whipped cream on top. Repeat these layers and end up again with whipped cream on top. Serves 8 to 10. Forget the calories and enjoy!

Heavenly Meringue Cake

Cake

½ cup butter, softened
½ cup sugar
4 egg yolks
¼ cup half-and-half
½ teaspoon vanilla extract
1 cup cake flour, sifted
1 ¼ teaspoons baking powder
⅛ teaspoon salt

In a large bowl cream butter and sugar. Add yolks, 1 at a time, beating after each addition. Add half-and-half and vanilla extract. In a small bowl sift flour, baking powder, and salt. Incorporate into wet mixture. Beat for 2 minutes. Foil base of two 9-inch layer cake pans. Grease and flour foil. Spread batter into pans.

Meringue

4 egg whites
Pinch of salt
1 cup sugar
1 teaspoon vanilla extract
¼ cup walnuts or pecans, chopped

Preheat oven to 350 degrees F. In medium bowl beat egg whites and salt til stiff. Gradually add sugar followed by vanilla extract. Beat for 1 minute. Spread meringue on top of cake batter in pans. Make sure the meringue is in uneven peaks and touches the edges of cake pans all around. On one of the layers sprinkle chopped nuts. Bake for 35 minutes. Allow cakes to cool in pans on wire racks.

Filling

½ pound dried apricots
2 cups water
Sugar to taste
½ cup cream, whipped

In small saucepan cook apricots in water over medium heat, simmering uncovered til tender, about 25 minutes. Add sugar to taste (about ¾ to 1 cup). Boil about 5 minutes then mash the fruit. Cool thoroughly and fold in whipped cream.

Assemble cake, place 1 layer meringue side down. Spread filling on layer. Place layer with nuts meringue side up on top of filling. Serves 8 to 10.

Mandarin Meringues

2 egg whites
¼ teaspoon cream of tartar
½ cup sugar
2 (11-ounce) cans mandarin orange sections
1 tablespoon sugar
1 ½ teaspoons cornstarch
1 tablespoon lemon juice
¼ teaspoon ground ginger

Bring egg whites to room temperature. In large bowl beat egg whites and cream of tartar til soft peaks form. Gradually add ½ cup sugar, and beat again til very stiff peaks form and sugar is dissolved.

Preheat oven to 275 degrees F. Cover a baking sheet with brown paper. Draw four circles on paper, each about 4 inches in diameter. Spread each with meringue, shaping into shells with back of spoon. Bake for 1 hour. Turn off heat and let shells dry in oven with door closed for 1 to 2 hours. Set aside.

Drain orange sections, reserving ½ cup syrup. Combine remaining sugar, cornstarch, and reserved syrup. Cook and stir til thickened. Stir in oranges, lemon juice, and ginger. Spoon orange mixture into meringue shells. Chill. Serves 4.

Mousse Au Kirsch

8 egg yolks
2 tablespoons vanilla extract
½ cup powdered sugar
2 cup heavy cream
2 cups milk
5 tablespoons Kirshwasser

In a large bowl beat eggs til frothy. Beat in powdered sugar a little at a time. In saucepan combine 1 cup cream with 1 cup milk and heat. Do not boil. Stir in vanilla extract. At the first sign of a simmer, remove mixture from heat. Allow to cool til it is lukewarm.

Stir beaten egg yolks into milk mixture. Set aside to cool thoroughly. Stir frequently while it cools. Add the remaining cup of cream and milk. Blend well.

Pour into freezer trays and let freeze til just firm. It must still be creamy and not too hard. Check every 30 minutes. While freezing, chill a large mixing bowl. Empty the frozen mousse into the chilled bowl. Add the Kirshwasser. Beat well, but quickly, and spoon into large individual parfait glasses. Top with chopped nuts and add a maraschino cherry on top each. Serves 6.

Oriental Crackling Fruit

2 cups sugar
½ cup honey
½ cup water
1 quart water
1 tray ice cubes
4 naval oranges, peeled and segmented
12 strawberries
4 red apples, cored and cut into 8 sections

In saucepan stir together sugar, honey, and ½ cup water. Bring to boil and continue to boil til a small amount dropped into cold water forms a hard ball (300 degrees F on candy thermometer). Put 1 quart water and ice in a shallow bowl. Spear fruit onto bamboo skewers.

Dip skewers into hot syrup, coating fruit thinly, and plunge fruit into ice water. Remove quickly and placed on a chilled serving plate. Serve at once. This may be done at the table. Spear individual fruit for dipping and eating. Serves 8.

Spanish Custard

1 ¾ cups whipping cream
1 cup milk
Pinch of salt
½ vanilla bean, split lengthwise
1 cup sugar
⅓ cup water
3 large eggs
2 egg yolks
7 tablespoons sugar

Combine cream, milk, and salt in medium saucepan. Scrape seeds from vanilla bean into mixture. Add bean. Bring to simmer over medium heat. Remove and let steep for 30 minutes. Combine 1 cup sugar and ⅓ cup water in another medium pan. Stir over low heat til sugar dissolves. Increase heat to high and cook without stirring til it is a deep amber color. Brush down sides of pan with wet pastry brush and swirl pan occasionally, about 10 minutes. Quickly pour caramel mix into 6 ramekins.

Preheat oven to 350 degrees F. Using hot pad, tilt each ramekin to coat sides. Set cups into baking pan. Whisk egg yolks and 7 tablespoons sugar in medium bowl til blended. Gradually and gently whisk cream mix into egg mix without creating a lot of foam. Pour custard through sieve into prepared ramekins. Add water to baking pan half way up sides of ramekins. Bake til set, about 40 minutes. Cool and continue to chill for about 2 hours. Serves 6 to 8.

Strawberry Lemon Meringue Nests

Make meringue and lemon curd up to 3 days ahead and then assemble just before serving.

3 large lemons
1 tablespoon cornstarch
6 tablespoons butter
1 ¼ cups sugar
4 large eggs, separated
¼ teaspoon cream of tartar
½ cup whipping cream
1 pint strawberries, hulled and cut into quarters
1 tablespoon strawberry preserves
Mint leaves for garnish

From lemons, grate 1 tablespoon of lemon peel and squeeze ½ cup juice. In 2-quart saucepan with wire whisk mix cornstarch, lemon peel, and juice til smooth.

Add butter and ¾ cup sugar. Heat to boiling over medium heat. Boil 1 minute, while stirring constantly.

In small bowl beat egg yolks slightly. Into yolks beat small amount of hot lemon mixture. Pour egg mixture back into lemon mix in saucepan and beat rapidly to prevent lumping.

Reduce heat to low and cook while stirring constantly, til mixture is thick, for about 5 minutes.

Pour lemon curd into medium bowl, cover surface with plastic wrap, and refrigerate for at least 3 hours or til well-chilled (can be refrigerated up to 3 days).

Meanwhile, prepare meringue nests. Preheat oven to 225 degrees F. Line large cookie sheet with foil. In small bowl with mixer at high speed, beat egg whites and cream of tartar til soft peaks form.

Sprinkle in ½ cup sugar, 2 tablespoons at a time, beating well after each addition til sugar dissolves and whites stand in stiff, glossy peaks.

Spoon meringue into 6 mounds on cookie sheet. With back of spoon, form a well in the center of each mound to create a nest. Bake nests 2 ½ hours.

Turn off oven and let nests remain in oven 1 hour to dry. Cool nests on cookie sheet on wire rack. If not using right away, store in an airtight container.

Just before serving, beat whipping cream at medium speed til stiff peaks form. Gently fold whipped cream into lemon curd.

In medium bowl toss strawberries with preserves. Spoon lemon-curd mix into meringue nests. Top with strawberry mix. Garnish with mint. Serves 6.

Breakfast Dishes

MEMORABLE MEALS

Dining During Delivery ◇ Other Blessed Events

The year was 1954, and Dittie was pregnant with our first child. The baby was due around Thanksgiving, but it was not until 4:00 a.m. on December 5 when Dittie woke me to say we should get to the hospital. Her little bag with gown, robe, and toothbrush had been waiting by the front door for about two weeks, so no time was lost in getting out the door.

The hospital was about twelve miles away, and as we drove we turned on the radio to take our minds off the coming event. We tuned into a popular radio drama and became interested in the story during the twenty minute ride. Dittie's labor pains had slowed down when we arrived and she suggested we wait to hear the final few minutes of the story. That we did. After the story ended, we proceeded in, got Dittie registered and admitted, and she was wheeled away.

I was allowed to spend a few minutes with her before they shooed me out so they could prep her for delivery. I was duly escorted to the waiting room where I found other expectant fathers. I was assured everything was going fine and within a few hours I would be a father. They also suggested I could wait in the cafeteria with some coffee and a roll. In those days, no one except the doctor and the hospital staff were allowed in the delivery room—especially not the father. I knew there was an all-night diner just a block or two away where I could get a better breakfast and perhaps kill more than a few minutes of the anticipated hours of waiting time.

I am sure by now you have guessed the ending of this story. When I returned to the hospital after about one half hour I was informed I was the father of a healthy baby boy. I was flabbergasted that the delivery had been so quick and rushed to my wife's side. Mother and child were doing well, and Dittie was so happy she forgot to be mad at me, although she never let me forget I had "deserted her" in her hour of need. We named him Charles Robert after our brothers.

After our first son's birth, this announcement (right) was hastily dispatched to friends and relatives.

```
THE 1954 "BABY BOY" MODEL NUMBER 1
21 INCH CHASSIE, WEIGHT 8 POUNDS 6 OUNCES
            CHARLES ROBERT
DELIVERED F.O.B. AT FAIRVIEW PARK HOSPITAL
            CLEVELAND, OHIO

    DESIGNER AND CHIEF ENGINEER
            DON McELWAIN
        PRODUCTION MANAGER
         DITTIE JO McELWAIN
        TECHNICAL ASSISTANT
          DR. E. R. SAUNDERS

   MODEL RELEASED - DECEMBER 5, 1954
2 LUNG POWER, FREE SQUEALING, SCREAMLINE
BODY, COLOR - CUSTOMARY PINK, FOCUSING HEAD-
LIGHTS, EQUIPPED WITH BLACK OUT BLINKERS,
ECONOMICAL SUCTION FEED, WATER COOLED
EXHAUST, CHANGEABLE SEAT COVERS.
    DUE TO EXISTING PRIORITY RATING ON
THIS MODEL, THE MANAGEMENT ASSURES THE
PUBLIC THERE WILL BE NO NEW MODELS RE-
LEASED DURING THE BALANCE OF THE YEAR.
```

Two and a half years after Chic was born, Dittie was pregnant with our second addition to the family. During her pregnancy, I had told Dittie several times that I knew I would love the new baby, but it would never have the same place in my heart as Chic. Again, as with Chic, her due date was late April and here it was May 9, and still no baby. The doctor decided he should induce labor. I was allowed to stay with her until the doctor thought delivery was getting near and then was again shooed out to the waiting room. This time there was no thought of going out for breakfast, lunch, or even a sweet roll, but there was coffee.

After a few hours I was informed we had a baby girl and asked if I knew what her name was to be. I told them it was Molly Jo. Molly was Dittie's grandmother's name and Jo, of course, was Dittie's middle name. Grandma spelled her name Mollie, but by the time my error was discovered, Molly's birth certificate was complete. Following Molly's birth I passed out cigars and candy at work. A secretary, also a mother, said it was too bad the girl was not the eldest as she could have helped care for the baby. An unmarried secretary, nearing forty, said it was nice that the baby would have an older brother who could introduce her to his male friends in later years. I guess it all depends on your point of view.

Molly always seemed to want to learn about things. Perhaps this is what led her to engineering. Anyway, once when she was about seven or eight we had grapefruit for breakfast, and after taking a seed from her mouth she asked if it would grow if she planted it. Her mother took a small flower pot, filled it with potting soil, and said, "Let's see." Molly poked a hole in the dirt, dropped the seed in, covered it, and added water. After a few days of patient care, a small shoot came up, and a tree was born. As the tree grew, the pot size was increased accordingly. After several years the tree was about 6 feet tall, the pot was about 2 feet in diameter, and the combination weighed an estimated 200 pounds. The tree thrived in the summer sun, but since we lived in upstate New York the tree could not stay outside during the winter, so we would bring it in. The size of the tree became limited by the size of the pot and, after about forty years, it is still taken outside each spring and brought into the basement before frost in the autumn.

It is probably unnecessary to say, but within two weeks Molly had me wrapped around her little finger. She held the same place in my heart that Chic did. I learned that love takes up no room in the heart; there is always room for more. I am sure Molly could still wrap me around her finger if she wanted. I never repeated that silly statement, not even eight years later when we discovered Dittie was pregnant again.

Nine years and three days after Molly was born, a different doctor also decided he should induce labor since Dittie was again two weeks overdue. The routine was the same as with Molly, but I do not recall having any coffee or donuts. I was not invited into the delivery room, although by 1966, it may have been permitted if I had argued. We were blessed with another boy who we named Andrew Walter. Andrew was the name of a McElvain who was an immigrant from Ireland in 1719 and may have (or may not have) been a direct ancestor. Walter was the name of Dittie's father.

It was like starting a new family all over again. This time, the prediction of the first secretary came true since Molly, age nine, all but adopted the new baby as her own live doll to be fussed over, bathed, fed, dressed, and rocked to sleep. She had no need for her toy dolls anymore, and they became part of Dittie's collection.

Andy was the athlete of the family. I liked to play golf and could usually shoot a little better than bogie golf. One day when he was about thirteen, I gave him Dittie's clubs and we went to a driving range, where he found he could hit the ball. Then we went to a small nine-hole course that was usually not very busy. We played one round and then went in for a soda and hot dog. I offered to play a second round; I would spot him one stroke per hole for the follow-up drink. As you can guess, it was a bad bet on my part; he beat me scratch. I never bet against him again in any sport. He is still a better than average bowler and golfer.

And now to breakfast:

Apple Coffee Cake

2 medium tart apples, peeled and chopped
13-ounce tube buttermilk biscuits
1 egg
1 tablespoon butter, softened
⅓ cup corn syrup
⅓ cup packed brown sugar
½ teaspoon cinnamon
½ cup chopped pecans

Preheat oven to 350 degrees F. Place 1 ½ cups chopped apples in greased 9-inch baking pan.

Separate biscuits into 10 pieces. Cut each biscuit into quarters and place over apples with point side up. Top with remaining apples.

In medium mixing bowl combine egg, corn syrup, brown sugar, butter, and cinnamon. Stir in pecans and spoon over apples. Bake for 30 to 35 minutes.

For glaze combine ⅓ cup powdered sugar, ¼ teaspoon vanilla extract, and 1 ½ teaspoons milk in medium bowl. Drizzle over warm cake. Serves 8 to 10.

Brunch For The Bunch

½ pound dried chip beef
6 ounces canned, sliced mushrooms
¼ cup butter
¼ cup bacon drippings
½ cup flour
1 quart milk
16 eggs
½ teaspoon salt
1 cup evaporated milk
¼ cup butter
Thinly sliced tomatoes for garnish

Tear or cut beef into manageable pieces. Drain and save mushroom juice. Heat butter and drippings in large skillet over medium heat. Add beef and mushrooms. Heat while stirring well to coat.

Sprinkle with flour and pepper and continue to heat, stirring til slightly crisped. Add milk and mushroom juice. Continue to cook and stir til smooth and slightly thick.

Preheat oven to 325 degrees F. Reheat cream mixture and grease 3-quart casserole. Beat eggs with fork and stir in salt and evaporated milk.

Melt butter in skillet and add eggs. Cook slowly til barely thickened, but not firm. Remove from heat.

Stir ¾ cup sauce gently into eggs and place in casserole dish. Pour hot cream mixture on top. Garnish with tomatoes. Place in oven til serving. Serves 10 to 12.

Dutch's Coffee Cake

1 egg
½ cup milk
½ cup sugar
3 teaspoons baking powder
4 tablespoons butter, softened
1 ½ cups flour
½ teaspoon salt

Preheat oven to 350 degrees F. In large bowl beat egg. Add sugar, butter, and milk. In a small bowl sift flour, baking powder, salt, and add to egg mixture. Pour into 8 x 8-inch pan and top with brown sugar mixed til crumbly with butter and cinnamon. Bake for 20 minutes. Serves 4.

EGG CASSEROLE

½ cup butter
½ cup flour
1 cup cream
1 cup milk
¼ teaspoon thyme
¼ teaspoon marjoram
¼ teaspoon basil
1 pound grated medium cheddar cheese
18 hard boiled eggs, sliced
1 pound bacon, cooked and crumbled
¼ cup parsley
Buttered bread crumbs

In medium saucepan melt butter. Blend in flour, cream, and milk gradually. Cook over medium heat and stir til thick. Add herbs. Add cheese and stir til melted.

Preheat oven to 350 degrees F. Place layer of eggs in greased casserole dish. Sprinkle some bacon on eggs, then parsley, and add a layer of sauce. Repeat 1 to 2 more times. Sprinkle top with bread crumbs. Bake uncovered for 30 minutes. Serves 10 to 12.

FRENCH TOAST

¼ cup flour
1 egg
½ cup milk

In shallow bowl whisk flour, egg, and milk. Dip four bread slices into batter, coating thoroughly.

Fry bread 2 at a time in large skillet over medium heat til browned on bottom. Flip and brown other side, about 4 minutes on each side. Cook thoroughly to ensure egg in middle is not raw.

Sprinkle with powdered sugar and cinnamon, if desired. Serves 2.

JEWISH COFFEE CAKE

1 package white or yellow cake mix
1 package instant vanilla pudding
½ cup oil
4 eggs
1 cup sour cream

In large bowl mix ingredients together for 5 minutes.

Cinnamon Topping

⅓ cup sugar
1 tablespoon cinnamon
1 teaspoon cocoa
½ cup chopped nuts

Preheat oven to 350 degrees F. Mix together topping ingredients and sprinkle ⅓ mix on bottom of cake pan and pour into greased tube pan. Swirl ⅔ of mixture into cake. Bake cake for 45 to 50 minutes. Serves 6 to 8.

MORNING COFFEE CAKE

4 eggs
1 cup sugar
1 cup oil
2 cups flour
1 teaspoon baking powder
½ teaspoon salt
1 teaspoon vanilla extract
1 can pie filling
Cinnamon-sugar to taste

Preheat oven to 350 degrees F. In large bowl beat eggs well. Gradually add sugar, oil, flour, baking powder, salt, and vanilla extract.

Spoon ½ of the batter into a greased 13 x 9-inch pan. Carefully spoon pie filling over batter. Carefully add the rest of the batter. Sprinkle with cinnamon-sugar.

Bake for 35 minutes. Serves 6 to 8.

MUSH

1 cup cornmeal
1 teaspoon salt

In large saucepan boil 3 cups water. In mixing bowl combine cornmeal, 1 cup cold water, and salt. Pour into boiling water. Cook while stirring til mixture becomes thick.

Cover and cook 10 minutes on low heat. Pour into loaf pans. Refrigerate.

When ready to eat slice into 1-inch thick slices and fry in skillet over medium heat til golden brown on each side, about 4 minutes per side. Serves 6 to 8.

PUMPKIN PIE COFFEE CAKE

1 package yellow cake mix
1 stick butter at room temperature
4 eggs
15 ounces canned pumpkin
5 ounces evaporated milk
1 ¼ cup sugar
2 teaspoons cinnamon
4 tablespoons chilled butter
1 cup chopped pecans
Whipped cream

Lightly grease and flour 13 x 9-inch cake pan. Reserve 1 cup cake mix. In large bowl blend the remaining cake mix, butter, and 1 egg on low speed for 1 minute.

Press batter over bottom of pan so it reaches the sides.

Filling

Using same bowl and beaters, blend the pumpkin, milk, 1 cup sugar, 3 eggs, and cinnamon on medium speed for 2 to 3 minutes. Mixture should be well-combined.

Pour over crust and spread to sides of pan. Mix ¼ cup sugar, chilled butter, and reserved cake mix in clean bowl with clean, dry beaters on low speed til crumbly. Stir in pecans. Distribute evenly over filling.

Bake til center no longer jiggles, 70 to 75 minutes. Cool on wire rack for 20 minutes. Refrigerate covered and serve with sweetened whipped cream. Serves 18 to 20.

SAUSAGE & EGG CASSEROLE

8 slices bread, cubed
1 ½ pounds pork sausage, browned and drained
2 cups grated cheddar cheese
4 ounces mushrooms, drained
4 eggs beaten
¾ teaspoon dry mustard
3 cups milk
1 can mushroom soup

Place cubed bread in greased 13 x 9-inch baking pan. Layer sausage over the bread. Sprinkle cheese and mushrooms on top.

In large bowl combine beaten eggs, mustard, and 2 ½ cup milk. Pour over top of ingredients in pan. Cover and refrigerate 3 hours or overnight.

When ready to bake, preheat oven to 300 degrees F. Combine soup and ½ cup milk and pour over all. Bake for 90 minutes. Serves 12.

Casseroles

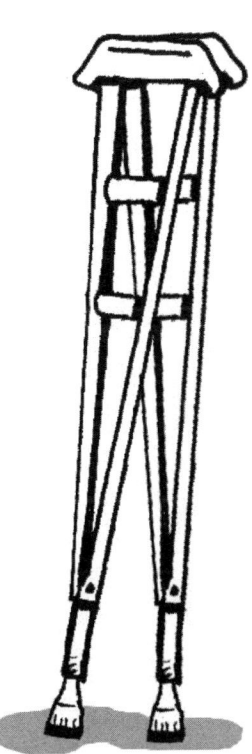

A Nibble of Prayer

Comfort Food ◊ Learning to Walk

When our son Charles (a.k.a. Chic, at that time) was very young he was constantly running everywhere. Furthermore, he did not always look where he was going. For example, one day when he was about five he ran around the corner of the house and onto the driveway—right into the front grill of Grandma's car. The car had been parked there for about an hour. He suffered only some minor scrapes and bumps, but when he came into the house crying he gave his Grandmother an accusing look and sobbed, "Why did you park your car there?"

It was a couple of years later Chic learned the hard way that it was sometimes better to walk than run. By this time he was in second grade. He was not allowed to run in the halls at school, which only seemed to give him more reason to run when he got home. One day he ran out of the back door, past the flowerbed, and was on his way to the driveway. In his haste, however, he failed to notice the garden hose by the bed and tripped on it. He landed face down atop a broken spade handle, partially sunk into the ground at the corner of the flowerbed to keep the hose from being dragged across it.

Dittie heard him cry and rushed out to him. There was no question he was hurt, so Dittie got him into the house and onto the sofa and tried to make him comfortable. He was there when I got home from work about a half hour later. We mutually agreed we should take him to the hospital Emergency Room. When we got there, he was immediately put into a bed by the ER nurse and the doctor on duty was summoned at once. After what seemed like forever, the doctor came to see us. He told us he thought Chic should stay overnight for observation because he had detected signs of internal bleeding and he was not sure of the extent of internal damage. We agreed and went home. That night we said a special prayer for him.

The next morning we were told the bleeding had not stopped and there was apparent damage to the liver and gall bladder area. They recommended exploratory surgery to assess the full extent of damage. We agreed and surgery was scheduled for the following morning.

As a result of the surgery, they determined his liver had been ruptured and displaced. There was additional damage that involved the gall bladder and, I believe, the pancreas. They had been able to repair it to what they felt was a satisfactory condition. In the following days, however, he was not recovering but was starting to run a high fever. After a week, his temperature was running up in the range of 104 and 105 and they knew they would have to operate again to isolate the new problem. They did, and it evolved that in the first operation they had used a gel-foam product to absorb any remnant blood and pass it out of the system. This was apparently standard practice in such cases. It turned out, however, Chic was allergic to the substance and it was creating an infection. Following the second operation, in which they cleaned out all the gel, he was still running a high fever for a couple of days, and we feared we might be losing him.

A friend of Chic's Grandmother had a part-time maid, and when she heard about Chic she said her church group would pray for the sick little boy that night. The following morning his fever broke. Within a couple of days he came home, and soon after that he was back in school.

I have always associated casseroles with church gatherings. It could be called comfort food.

BAKED SICILIAN STYLE ZITI

1 pound ziti
1 large eggplant
1 pound mozzarella, grated
3 cups spaghetti sauce
1 cup grated Parmesan cheese

Cook ziti following package directions. Slice eggplant into thin strips and sauté in a large skillet with ¼ cup olive oil til soft.

Preheat oven to 350 degrees F. Cover bottom of 13 x 9-inch pan with 1 cup spaghetti sauce, followed by a layer of ziti, mozzarella cheese, and then the cooked eggplant. Sprinkle with Parmesan and more sauce. Repeat layers, covering top with remaining sauce. Bake for 30 minutes. Serve immediately. Serves 8 to 10.

CHEESY TACO BAKE

1 pound ground beef
1 can tomato soup
1 cup chunky salsa
½ cup milk
6 flour or 8 corn tortillas cut into 1-inch pieces
1 cup shredded cheddar cheese

Preheat oven to 400 degrees F. In large skillet over medium heat, brown beef. Add soup, salsa, milk, tortillas, and half of the cheese. Stir til combined and spoon into a 2-quart baking dish. Cover with aluminum foil. Bake for 30 minutes. Sprinkle with remaining cheese. Serves 4 to 6.

CHICKEN & DRESSING

8 ounces packaged stuffing
3 to 4 uncooked chicken breasts, cubed
½ cup margarine
Pepper to taste
6 eggs
½ cup flour
4 cups chicken broth
3 teaspoons salt
1 cup cream of chicken soup

Preheat oven to 325 degrees F. Prepare stuffing per package directions and spread on bottom of 13 x 9-inch pan. Top with chicken. In medium saucepan over low heat melt margarine with flour, add broth til thick. In large bowl, beat eggs and then add a little of the broth to the eggs. Add egg and broth mixture to the remainder of the broth to make gravy. Add soup and pour custard over chicken. Bake for 1 hour. Serves 4.

CHICKEN CASSEROLE

½ cup noodles, cooked per package directions
2 tablespoons butter
2 tablespoons flour
1 cup milk or chicken broth
½ teaspoon salt
⅛ teaspoon pepper
¼ teaspoon celery seed
1 cup cooked cubed chicken
2 hard boiled eggs, diced
½ cup chopped green pepper
½ cup grated cheese
½ cup sliced mushrooms

Preheat oven to 375 degrees F. Combine flour, butter, milk or broth, celery seed, salt, and pepper in large mixing bowl to make a sauce. In separate bowl combine chicken and drained noodles, diced eggs, green pepper, and mushrooms. Toss gently. Place in 2-quart casserole dish. Sprinkle with grated cheese and add sauce and mix. Top with buttered bread crumbs.

Bake for 30 minutes. If refrigerated bake at 350 degrees F for 60 minutes. If frozen bake at 325 degrees F for 90 minutes. Serves 4.

Chipped Beef Casserole

2 cups noodles, cooked per package directions
2 tablespoons flour
2 tablespoons butter, melted
1 cup milk
¼ pound cheddar cheese spread
¼ pound chipped beef, cut small
Grated cheddar cheese for topping

Preheat oven to 350 degrees F. In medium skillet over medium heat sauté chipped beef. In large mixing bowl combine flour, milk, and melted butter to make white sauce. Melt ¼ pound cheese in saucepan, stirring over low heat, and pour into white sauce. Add chipped beef and stir to coat evenly.

Pour into 2-quart greased casserole dish and sprinkle with grated cheese. Bake for 30 minutes F. Spiced beef is less salty than chipped beef. To decrease salt in chipped beef, pour boiling water over it, let stand 1 minute, and drain before you sauté it. Serves 4 to 6.

Chicken Broccoli Casserole

4 to 5 cups cubed cooked chicken
3 packages frozen chopped broccoli, cooked
2 cans chicken soup
1 cup mayonnaise
1 teaspoon lemon juice
½ teaspoon curry powder
1 cup grated sharp cheese
Box of stuffing mix, prepared

Preheat oven to 350 degrees F. In large bowl combine soup, mayonnaise, lemon juice, curry powder, and cheese to make sauce. In 13 x 9-inch pan, place a layer of broccoli, then chicken, and cover with sauce. Sprinkle prepared stuffing over top of casserole. Bake for 30 minutes. Serves 8.

Country Club Chipped Beef

2 large jars chipped beef
1 package frozen artichoke hearts, cooked and drained
2 tablespoons flour
2 tablespoons butter
1 tablespoon grated Parmesan cheese
1 ½ cups sour cream
1 can mushroom soup
1 can mushrooms
2 tablespoons butter
Rice chex, ½ cup per serving

Melt butter in small saucepan over low heat. Mix together butter, flour, sour cream, cheese, soup, and mushrooms in large saucepan. Shred chipped beef and pour boiling water over it. Let drain. Add beef and artichokes to saucepan mixture. Cook slowly for 15 minutes or til warmed throughout.

Preheat oven to 350 degrees F. Spread rice chex on cookie sheet. Brush with 2 tablespoons melted butter. Place in oven until golden brown. Place browned corn and rice cereal in large casserole dish and cover with beef mixture. Serves 6 to 8.

Crab & Shrimp Casserole

1 medium green pepper, chopped
1 medium onion, chopped
1 cup chopped celery
6 ½ ounces crab
6 ½ ounces shrimp
½ teaspoon salt
Pepper to taste
1 teaspoon Worchester sauce
1 cup mayonnaise
1 cup buttered bread crumbs

Preheat oven to 350 degrees F. Combine all ingredients. Pour into 1 ½-quart casserole dish, and bake for 30 minutes. Serves 6 to 8.

CRAB MEAT MOUSSE

2 packages lemon gelatin
2 cups hot water
1 cup cold water
Juice of 1 lemon
½ cup slivered almonds
¼ teaspoon salt
1 cup mayonnaise
2 cans crab

Pour hot water in large bowl over gelatin and mix til dissolved. Add cold water, lemon juice, and salt. Add mayonnaise and beat well. Let mixture cool and add remaining ingredients and mold. Serves 6.

GOURMET CASSEROLE

8 ounces thin noodles, prepared
½ cup chopped onions
2 tablespoons butter
2 pounds ground beef
¾ cup olives, sliced once
1 can mushroom soup
1 cup chow mein noodles
1 soup can filled with milk
½ pound grated cheddar cheese
1 tablespoon thyme
1 tablespoon chives
½ pound slivered blanched almonds

Preheat oven to 350 degrees F. Cook noodles in salted water and drain. In large skillet sauté onions in butter and set aside. In same skillet brown beef and add onions, olives, soup, milk, herbs, and cheese. Add onions and noodles to mixture and combine gently. Spoon into greased 2-quart casserole dish. Bake mixture in a shallow casserole to get the maximum amount of topping.

Bake covered for 30 minutes. Remove cover. Sprinkle with mixed almonds and chow mein noodles. This topping is especially good. Bake covered for 20 minutes more. Serves 10.

GREEN RICE CASSEROLE

2 cups cooked rice
¾ cup uncooked rice
1 cup grated sharp cheddar cheese
¼ cup melted butter
2 tablespoons chopped onion
1 cup chopped parsley
3 beaten egg yolks
3 stiffly beaten egg whites
Salt and pepper to taste

Preheat oven to 350 degrees F. In large mixing bowl combine all ingredients, except egg whites. Blend in beaten egg whites and place in greased 13 x 9-inch baking dish. Bake for 35 minutes. Serve with creamed crab or shrimp. Serves 6. Can use cream of mushroom soup as a sauce.

HAM & BROCCOLI CASSEROLE

2 packages chopped broccoli, cooked
1 ½ cups grated cheddar cheese
2 cups chopped ham

In a 13 x 9-inch dish layer broccoli first, then cheese and ham.

1 cup biscuit mix
⅓ cup milk
4 eggs

Preheat oven to 350 degrees F. Combine ingredients in mixing bowl and beat til smooth and pour over the above layers. Bake for 1 hour. Serves 6.

Heavenly Onion Casserole

2 tablespoons butter
3 medium sweet Spanish onions, sliced
8 ounces fresh mushrooms, sliced
4 ounces shredded Swiss cheese
1 can mushroom soup, undiluted
1 can evaporated milk
2 teaspoons soy sauce
6 to 8 slices French bread, ½-inch thick
6 to 8 slices Swiss cheese

In large skillet melt butter over medium heat and sauté onions and mushrooms til tender. Place in 12 x 7-inch baking dish. Sprinkle shredded Swiss cheese on top.

In a separate bowl combine soup, milk, and soy sauce. Pour over shredded cheese. Top with bread and cheese slices. Cover and refrigerate at least 4 hours, but overnight is better.

Preheat oven to 375 degrees F. Bake loosely covered for 30 minutes. Uncover and bake for 15 to 20 minutes. Let stand 5 minutes before serving. Serves 6 to 8. Chunks of ham make a nice addition to casserole.

Hot Tuna Casserole

1 large can tuna
1 can mushroom soup
1 can celery soup
1 small cup blanched almonds
1 teaspoon soy sauce
1 small onion
½ green pepper, chopped
1 tablespoon pimentos
1 medium can chow mein noodles

Preheat oven to 325 degrees F. Reserve some chow mein noodles for topping. In a large bowl mix everything else together except almonds. Spoon into 13 x 9-inch casserole dish. Sprinkle reserved noodles and almonds on top.

Bake for 35 to 45 minutes. Serves 8.

Holupki Casserole

1 head cabbage, shredded and partially cooked
1 pound ground beef
½ cup rice (not instant) par boiled
1 egg
1 large onion, chopped
Salt and pepper to taste

In large skillet over medium heat sauté onion. In large bowl mix onion, beef, rice, egg, salt, and pepper.

Sauce

16 ounces stewed tomatoes
1 can tomato soup
1 tablespoon fresh dill
Salt and pepper to taste

Preheat oven to 350 degrees F. In large bowl combine sauce ingredients. Refill soup can with water and add to sauce mixture.

In 13 x 9-inch casserole dish layer cabbage, followed by meat mixture and sauce. Cover tightly with foil. Bake for 90 minutes. Serves 6.

Quiche Lorraine

9-inch pie crust
1 small onion, chopped
3 strips bacon, diced
½ pound grated Swiss cheese
2 cups light cream
4 eggs, well-beaten
1 tablespoon butter, melted
½ teaspoon nutmeg
Salt and pepper to taste
Dash of hot sauce

Place crust in 9-inch pie pan. In medium skillet over medium heat sauté bacon and onion til brown. Sprinkle onion and bacon into uncooked pie shell.

Preheat oven to 400 degrees F. In large bowl combine grated cheese, eggs, cream, melted butter, nutmeg, salt, pepper, and hot sauce.

Pour cheese mixture over bacon and onions in pie shell and bake for 15 minutes. Reduce heat to 350 degrees F and bake for 30 minutes more.

Cool at room temperature and cut into pie shaped wedges. Serves 6 to 8.

Ruben Casserole

1 cup sour cream
1 large onion, diced
1 large can or bag of sauerkraut, drained
1 can corn beef
12 to 16 ounces grated Swiss cheese
8 slices rye bread, crumbled
1 cup melted margarine

Preheat oven to 350 degrees F. In bowl combine onion and sour cream. Spread in bottom of a 13 x 9-inch pan.

Arrange sauerkraut over sour cream. Crumble corned beef over sauerkraut and sprinkle grated cheese over meat. Top with bread crumbs and drizzle butter over all.

Bake for 45 minutes. Serves 8.

Taco Casserole

10 taco shells
1 ½ pounds ground beef
1 ¼ ounces taco seasoning mix
½ cup water
2 tablespoons minced onion
8 ounces tomato sauce
2 cups grated Monterey jack cheese
1 large tomato, cut into wedges
6 green olives, sliced
Taco sauce

Lightly grease 1 ½-quart casserole dish. Crush 5 taco shells and sprinkle in bottom of dish. Crush remaining shells and set aside.

Preheat oven to 350 degrees F. In large skillet over medium heat, brown beef and then drain. Return to heat and add taco seasoning mix and water. Simmer uncovered for 10 minutes. Stir in onion and tomato sauce. Spoon meat mix over taco shells and top with ½ cup grated cheese.

Sprinkle remaining chips over cheese followed by remaining cheese. Arrange tomatoes and olives on top.

Bake for 15 to 20 minutes. Serves 10.

Tuna Chow Mein

½ can chow mein noodles
¾ cup salted cashews
1 tablespoon butter
1 can tuna, with liquid
1 cup diced celery
1 can mushroom soup
¼ cup chopped onion
2 tablespoons chopped green peppers
¼ cup milk
¼ cup water

Preheat oven to 350 degrees F. Melt butter in a large skillet over low heat. To butter add diced celery, mushroom soup, chopped onion, and chopped green peppers. Cook over medium-low heat while stirring til onion is tender.

Reserve ¼ cup noodles for topping. Mix in remaining noodles, cashews, milk, water, and tuna with liquid. Stir to combine and remove from heat. Pour mixture into 1 ½-quart casserole. Sprinkle reserved chow mein noodles over top.

Bake uncovered for 30 minutes. Serves 6 to 8.

Turkey Casserole

1 cup rice
1 can cream of chicken soup
1 can cream of celery soup
2 cups chicken or turkey

Preheat oven to 325 degrees F. Cook rice per package directions. In a medium mixing bowl combine turkey or chicken with chicken soup and celery soup. Stir rice into soup. Place mixture in 2-quart casserole dish in oven. Bake for 30 to 45 minutes.

Top casserole with French-fried onions and bake for 10 minutes more. Serves 4.

Seafood

BITTEN BY THE SEA

Aloha Vacation ◊ Long Awaited Getaway

Dittie and I both enjoyed the vacations we took each year. Often we would go somewhere with one of our parents, or visit them at home. What Dittie and I wanted most was to take a trip to Hawaii. We kept saying, "Maybe next year." Eventually, all three of our children were married and two of the three moved out of town, so they were added to our visiting list. The promised "next years" just seemed to keep coming and going, and we still did not get to Hawaii. We finally agreed we would go to Hawaii on our 25th anniversary in 1976. But that year, my work took me out of town, and we missed the opportunity. Again, we told ourselves, "Next year."

After we both retired in 1994 we saw a travel agent who arranged two weeks to be spent among three of the Hawaiian Islands. It was wonderful! We spent four days in Honolulu, lolling on Waikiki Beach, visiting the Arizona Memorial, and doing all the things offered for tourists on the island of Oahu. Then we visited the Kaanapali Beach area on Maui for four days where we thoroughly enjoyed more of the same. Then we finished our vacation at the King Kamehameha Hotel on the island of Hawaii. We visited the city of Hilo, the orchid capital of the world, saw an active volcano, stood ten feet from a small lava flow, and went snorkeling in Kealakekua Bay.

It was so great we wound up buying a two week time-share at the Kona Coast Resort. It was one of the best investments we ever made. We returned again in February of 1997, 1999, 2001, and 2003. In 1999 we brought two friends with us to share the condominium, and they enjoyed Hawaii so much, they also purchased two weeks at a different resort.

When we returned to Hawaii in 2001, we were celebrating our 50th anniversary year. At various functions we attended, the Emcee would often ask if any couples were celebrating an anniversary, and we always responded. We were frequently asked what the secret to such a long life together was. I would manage to offer some response, but I never had a really good answer until after we got home.

One of Dittie's hobbies was doing counted cross-stitch. She made several beautiful pictures and managed a lot of small samplers containing quotable sayings that covered a fair share of the kitchen wall. One of those samplers answered the questions better than anything I could have originated. It reads as follows:

All the fine compliments
All the good wishes
Will never replace
Help with the dishes!

Make a habit of kindness and consideration toward your mate, and the happy years by themselves will accumulate.

Although I have no recipes for Hawaiian dishes to offer, here are Dittie's seafood recipes:

CRABMEAT IN SHELLS

1 can king crab
1 can button mushrooms
2 tablespoons butter
2 tablespoons flour
½ cup chicken stock
½ cup cream
½ can mushroom soup
2 tablespoons lemon juice

Preheat oven to 350 degrees F. Combine ingredients in a large bowl and spoon into baking shells arranged on baking sheet. Salt and pepper lightly to taste.

Add shredded cheddar cheese to top of shells. Bake for 30 minutes. Serves 4.

CRAB NICHOLA

½ gallon milk
½ pound melted butter
2 cups flour
Salt and pepper to taste
Dash of sherry
1 cup finely diced green and red peppers
2 pounds Alaskan king crab
8 English muffins
16 tomato slices
8 American cheese slices
Paprika

Preheat oven to 350 degrees F. In medium skillet sauté red and green peppers. Melt butter in medium saucepan over low heat. Make a roux by slowly stirring in flour and then the milk. Heat, stirring constantly, til sauce thickens. Add red and green peppers, sherry, and crab. Stir thoroughly. Remove sauce from heat.

Split and toast English muffins. Place on baking sheet. Spoon a generous amount of sauce on each muffin and top with 2 tomato slices, an American cheese slice, and a sprinkle of paprika. Bake for about 10 to 15 minutes til cheese is lightly brown. Serves 8.

CRAB STUFFED MUSHROOMS

7 ½ ounces king crab
2 teaspoons chives
1 tablespoon sherry
1 teaspoon Worcestershire sauce
¼ teaspoon salt
Dash of white pepper
2 tablespoons butter
1 ½ tablespoons flour
½ cup milk
Salt and white pepper to taste
25 large mushroom caps

Chop crab. In large bowl combine crab, chives, sherry, Worcestershire sauce, ¼ teaspoon salt, and dash of white pepper.

Preheat oven to 350 degrees F. In saucepan melt butter over low heat. Add flour to melted butter and mix well. Add milk, salt, and white pepper. Cook and stir til thickened. Pour into crab mixture.

Place mushroom caps on baking sheet and fill with crab mixture and sprinkle with paprika. Bake for 10 to 15 minutes. Serves 10 to 12.

FISH MARINADE

½ teaspoon rosemary
¼ cup oil
2 tablespoons lemon juice
Salt and pepper to taste

In a shallow mixing bowl combine ingredients and let stand for 1 hour. Strain. Dip fish of choice into marinade and grill or broil for 5 to 8 minutes on each side.

GRILLED SALMON WITH LIME BUTTER

1 stick butter, melted
¼ cup lime juice
1 tablespoon pepper
4 salmon steaks, about 9 ounces each
Lime wedges

In medium bowl combine butter, lime juice, and pepper. Place salmon in glass baking dish and pour sauce on top of salmon. Let marinate while preheating broiler. Brush occasionally while broiling. Broil about 4 minutes per side. Before serving brush with remaining sauce. Serve with lime wedges. Serves 4.

REDFISH SUPREME

4 to 5 pounds redfish
1 teaspoon salt
½ teaspoon pepper
1 cup water
½ cup oil
1 ¼ sticks butter
8 tablespoons flour
2 tablespoons chopped onion
Pimento
1 cup chopped celery
½ cup chopped parsley
1 pound crab meat and shrimp
1 medium can mushrooms
½ stick butter
½ cup grated American cheese
Salt and pepper to taste

Preheat oven to 400 degrees F. Rub salt, pepper, and oil inside and outside of redfish. Place fish on rack over roaster and add water in bottom, don't let water touch fish.

Cover and cook 40 minutes, save drippings.

Sauce

Melt butter in large saucepan over low heat. Add flour and stir til golden brown. Add onion, celery, parsley, and pimento. Cook and stir about 5 minutes.

Remove from heat and add drippings from roaster, water from mushrooms, and enough extra water to make a smooth sauce.

Sauté mushrooms in butter in medium skillet over medium heat. Place fish in large flat baking dish, 3 to 4 inches deep.

Cover fish with sauce, mushrooms, crab, and shrimp. Sprinkle with cheese and bread crumbs.

Bake fish at 400 degrees F til brown, about 15 minutes. Serves 8.

ROMOULADE SAUCE

½ teaspoon mustard
2 tablespoons grated onion
1 pint mayonnaise
¼ cup horseradish
½ ounce chives
¼ teaspoon salt
1 tablespoon lemon
¼ teaspoon pepper

In large bowl mix all ingredients til well-combined. Refrigerate and allow to steep for a few hours, or even overnight. Serve on the side with cold broiled shrimp or fried fish.

Salmon with Lemon Chive Cream Sauce

¾ cup clam juice
⅓ cup dry white wine
¼ cup finely chopped shallots
1 tablespoon dry vermouth
½ cup whipping cream
1 tablespoon lemon juice
1 tablespoon chives
1 pound salmon, cut diagonally
2 tablespoons butter

Combine juice, wine, shallots, and vermouth in small saucepan. Boil over medium heat til liquid is reduced to ⅓ cup, about 10 minutes. Add cream, boil til sauce coats spoon, about 2 minutes. Add lemon, strain and return to pan but remove from heat. Add chives, salt, and pepper.

Cut salmon on deep diagonals into 8 strips, ¼-inch thick. Sprinkle with salt, pepper, and nutmeg. Melt butter in large skillet over medium heat. Add salmon to skillet and cook til opaque in center, about 30 seconds per side.

Return sauce to heat and bring to boil, pour on serving plate, and place salmon on top. Garnish with whole chives, if desired. Serves 4.

Scallops & Asparagus with Mushrooms

2 tablespoons oil
1 bunch asparagus cut into 1-inch pieces
½ pound Portobello mushrooms
3 cloves garlic, chopped
1 tablespoon cornstarch
1 pound scallops
¾ cup chicken broth
Juice of ½ a lemon

Heat 1 tablespoon oil in large skillet. Sauté scallops over medium-low heat til just cooked, remove from skillet. Add remaining oil to skillet and stir-fry asparagus, mushrooms, and garlic on medium-high heat til tender-crisp. Return scallops to skillet.

Combine broth and cornstarch, pour into skillet. Season with lemon juice, salt, and pepper. Simmer til sauce thickens and ingredients are heated throughout. Serves 4.

Shrimp Creole

2 tablespoons butter
¾ cup chopped onion
½ cup chopped celery
½ cup chopped green pepper
1 small garlic clove, minced
8 ounces tomato sauce
½ cup water
1 teaspoon parsley flakes
½ teaspoon salt
⅛ teaspoon cayenne pepper
1 bay leaf
1 cup raw shrimp
1 ½ cups cooked rice

Melt butter in large skillet over medium heat. Add onion, celery, green pepper, and garlic. Cook and stir til onion is tender.

Stir in tomato sauce, water, parsley flakes, and seasonings. Simmer uncovered for 20 minutes. Stir in shrimp. Heat to boiling, then reduce heat, cover, and simmer til shrimp are done, about 10 minutes. Serve over rice. Serves 2.

Seafood Chowder

1 ½ pound halibut, fresh or frozen
6 ounces frozen crab
3 medium potatoes
1 large Spanish onion
¾ cup chopped celery
¼ cup chopped green pepper
2 cloves garlic, minced
¼ teaspoon thyme
¼ teaspoon marjoram
Snipped parsley
¼ cup margarine
2 (16-ounce) cans tomatoes
2 cups clam tomato juice
1 ½ teaspoons salt
¼ teaspoon pepper
½ pound shrimp

Cut fish into 1-inch cubes. Drain crab and slice small. Peel potatoes and cut into ½-inch pieces. Slice onions thin.

Sauté onion, celery, peppers, and garlic in butter in large skillet over medium heat. Add tomatoes with liquid, clam tomato juice, and seasonings.

Add halibut and potatoes. Cover and simmer about 10 minutes.

Remove from heat, combine with shrimp and crab and sprinkle with parsley. Serves 8.

Tuna Lasagna

½ cup chopped onion
1 clove garlic
2—7 ounce cans tuna
10 ½ ounces cream of celery soup
½ cup milk
½ teaspoon oregano
¼ teaspoon pepper
½ pound lasagna noodles, cook as directed
½ pound sliced processed cheese
Grated Parmesan cheese

In large skillet sauté onion and garlic in oil til onion is softened. Add tuna, soup, milk, oregano, and pepper. Remove from heat and stir to combine into sauce. Preheat oven to 350 degrees F.

In 12 x 7-inch baking dish arrange layer of noodles on bottom. Cover noodles with tuna sauce followed by cheese slices. Continue alternating layers til you finish with layer of cheese. Sprinkle top layer with Parmesan cheese.

Bake for 30 minutes. Allow to stand for at least 5 minutes before serving. Serves 4 to 6.

Holiday Treats

Ceremonial Flavor

Through the Generations ◊ Christmas Tradition

When I was young, about four or five, I believed in Santa Claus because my Mom and Dad would talk about him. I was not in school yet where other kids may have dissuaded me from my belief. There was no television in the 1930s, so we did not have Santa Claus thrust upon us every few minutes, telling us to buy this or that toy. If there were Santas in department stores, I do not remember them. I was convinced Santa was real and he was somewhere, although I did not know what the North Pole was. I did know, however, he was the one who brought presents to good girls and boys.

In our family, Santa was Grandpa Vertner, complete with red suit, floppy pointed cap with a fur ball on the tip, false beard, and a natural belly that shook "like a bowl full of jelly" when he laughed. We knew he was not the real Santa Claus, but that was all right. To this day, whenever I see an old photo of Grandma Vertner, she looks to me like the depiction of Mrs. Claus. She had a rather plump figure and gray hair she always wore in a bun. I do not remember anyone telling me so, but I always thought the real Santa was busy delivering presents to children whose parents could not afford to buy any. We were happy we were not as unfortunate as that.

In many families it is a tradition at Christmas time to prepare a plate or tray of goodies to distribute to friends and neighbors. To my knowledge it has been a tradition in our family beginning with Dittie's mother, but I suspect that it began in her family at least one or more generations before that. We would normally select eight to ten different candies and cookies to make from the following groups. It would not necessarily be the same list every year; although there are some favorites that are always requested, as well as some that we would not pass over ourselves. A few pieces of each would be included on each plate, and if we knew which goodies were favored by a particular family we would try to lean a little heavier on those.

I know the tradition has been in our two generations for over fifty years, and I intend to continue it as long as I can. Our children also get out the recipe book each year to make some of their favorites. You should be able to find some of your favorites among the following recipes, and maybe some you have yet to try but sound like they may be good. They probably are.

Don's Christmas Treats ◇ by Michele Constable

During conversations with Don McElwain, I learned that one of his wife's practices was to give plates of homemade cookies and candies to friends at Christmas time. My mother had always done the same, and it is a tradition I also value. Don told me he wanted to continue his wife's custom. I admired him both for wanting to honor her in this way and having to learn how to make the treats before he could offer them.

Last Christmas Eve day, Don called me to see where I lived, so I also could receive a plate of his candy. I was both pleased and amazed when I saw what he brought—at least eight different things and all done perfectly. There were pressed cookies in Christmas shapes, chocolates, caramels, turtles—which Don seemed to be almost ashamed to admit how easy they were to make—and then there were the Buckeyes. Don and I are both Buckeyes, graduates of the Ohio State University. One Buckeye treat is candy buckeyes, chocolate covered peanut butter balls with some of the peanut butter left showing to resemble a buckeye. Don's were perfect. He had held them up with toothpicks to get an even chocolate coating and retain the round shape; an amateur would have tried to take shortcuts. His interest and ability has gone far beyond the basic lessons of the "Men Making Meals" classes.

OHIO BUCKEYES

1 ½ pounds powdered sugar, 6 cups
½ pound margarine or butter, softened
2 cups smooth peanut butter
¼ cup paraffin (honest), about ½ cake of paraffin

In large bowl mix powdered sugar, margarine, and peanut butter, chill for 1 hour. Roll mixture into bite-size pieces, and refrigerate overnight.

Next day, melt 6 ounces chocolate chips and 6 ounces butterscotch chips in double boiler. Over medium-low heat in saucepan melt paraffin, add to chocolate/butterscotch mixture and mix well. Hold balls with a toothpick and dip into melted mixture, leaving a small area exposed near the toothpick for the eye. NOTE: It works better if you remove only about 1 to 2 dozen peanut butter balls from the refrigerator at a time.

Invert the toothpick and stick it into a piece of Styrofoam covered with waxed paper and allow the chocolate to cool. When the chocolate is solid, remove the toothpicks and store the Buckeyes in an airtight container.

Makes 7 to 8 dozen candies.

Candies

Almond Rolls

⅔ cup canned blanched almonds, finely ground
½ cup margarine
½ cup sugar
2 tablespoons milk
1 tablespoon flour, sifted 4 times
Additional powdered sugar for garnish

Preheat oven to 350 degrees F. Grease and flour 2 cookie sheets. In large skillet, combine all ingredients over low heat and stir til butter is melted. Drop by heaping teaspoonfuls, 3 inches apart, on prepared cookie sheet.

Bake in oven 1 sheet at a time, about 5 to 6 minutes or til golden brown. Remove balls 1 at a time from cookie sheet and quickly roll up around handle of wooden spoon and set aside to cool. To serve, dust lightly with powdered sugar. Makes about 30 small almond rolls.

Apricot Fingers

12 ounces dried apricots
1 medium orange
1 ½ cups sugar

Squeeze 4 ounces juice from orange and set aside. Grind apricots and orange rind. Place in large heavy saucepan. Add juice and 1 ½ cups sugar. Stir or blend, the mixture will be thick. Bring to boiling point over low heat. Boil about 10 minutes, stirring constantly.

Place in mixing bowl and let cool for 1 hour or more, so you can handle it.

Place 1 cup sugar in a small bowl. Drop mixture a teaspoon at a time into sugar, coat evenly. Roll between your hands to make a finger shaped roll, dip in sugar occasionally.

Place on wax paper on baking tray. Allow to dry overnight.

Caramel Candy

1 pound brown sugar
1 can sweetened condensed milk
½ pound butter
1 cup corn syrup

Combine ingredients in large saucepan and cook til temperature reaches 245 degrees F, approximately 20 minutes, stirring constantly. Pour mixture into a buttered jelly roll pan. Cool and then cut into squares and wrap in plastic wrap or aluminum foil.

Caramel Corn

½ cup margarine
1 cup packed brown sugar
¼ cup white corn syrup
½ teaspoon salt
½ teaspoon vanilla extract
¼ teaspoon baking soda
3 quarts popcorn, popped

Preheat oven to 300 degrees F. In large saucepan melt margarine, sugar, corn syrup, and salt. Bring to a boil while stirring constantly, and boil without stirring for 5 minutes. Remove from heat and add baking soda and vanilla extract. Pour over popped corn. Mix well to coat evenly and spoon into 12 x 17-inch pan. Bake uncovered for 30 minutes, stir after 15 minutes. Remove and cool.

Chocolate Peanut Butter Cups

3 heaping tablespoons creamy peanut butter
1 pound candy making chocolate, melted

In medium bowl stir peanut butter into melted candy making chocolate. Mix well and pour into small candy cups. Allow to harden. Makes about 48 cups.

Coffee Walnut Toffee

2 ½ sticks unsalted butter
1 cup sugar
⅓ cup packed brown sugar
⅓ cup water
1 tablespoon dark molasses
3 teaspoon instant espresso powder
½ teaspoon cinnamon
¼ teaspoon salt
2 cups coarsely chopped toasted walnuts
4 ½ ounces chocolate chips
4 ½ ounces white chocolate, finely chopped

Butter a small cookie sheet. Melt the 2 ½ sticks of butter in 2 ½-quart pan over low heat. Add both sugars, water, molasses, espresso powder, cinnamon, and salt. Stir til sugar dissolves.

Using a candy thermometer increase heat to medium. Cook til thermometer measures 290 degrees F, stirring slowly but constantly, scraping bottom of pan with wooden spatula to keep mixture from sticking, about 20 minutes.

Remove from heat and add 1 ½ cups of nuts. Immediately pour in pan. Tilt sheet so toffee spreads to ¼-inch thick, sprinkle dark and white chocolates in checkerboard pattern on top. Let stand 1 minute. With back of a spoon swirl chocolate to spread lightly. Shake sheet to form even chocolate layer. Use tip of knife to swirl chocolate. Add remaining nuts. Refrigerate til firm, about 1 hour.

Fudgie Scotch Ring

6 ounces chocolate chips
6 ounces butterscotch chips
1 can sweetened condensed milk
1 cup chopped walnuts
½ teaspoon vanilla extract
1 cup walnut halves

Melt chocolate and butterscotch chips with condensed milk in top of double boiler over hot, but not boiling, water. Stir occasionally til chips melt and mixture begins to thicken. When well-blended, remove from heat and chill for 1 hour til mix thickens. Line bottom of 9-inch pie pan with a 12-inch square of foil. Place ¾ cup walnut halves in bottom of pan, forming a 2-inch wide ring.

Spoon chocolate mix in small amounts on top of walnuts to form ring. Decorate with remaining nuts. Chill in refrigerator til firm enough to slice into ½-inch slices.

Homemade Toffee Candy

2 sticks margarine
1 tablespoon white corn syrup
5 tablespoons water
1 teaspoon vanilla extract
¼ teaspoon salt
6 chocolate bars
½ cup chopped pecans

In large saucepan combine ingredients, except chocolate and nuts, and stir, stir, stir over medium heat. Boil to 300 degrees F. Pour into greased 13 x 9-inch pan. While hot cover with chocolate then sprinkle with nuts. Allow to harden then break into bite-size pieces.

Mom's Fudge

⅔ cup evaporated milk
7 ounces marshmallow crème
1 ⅓ cups sugar
¼ teaspoon salt
¼ cup butter

Mix ingredients in large saucepan over medium heat. Stir constantly and bring to a boil. Boil for 5 minutes. Grease 11 x 7-inch pan. Remove from heat and stir in 12 ounces chocolate chips til melted and smooth. Add 1 teaspoon vanilla extract and nuts, if desired.

Pour into greased pan. Can substitute butterscotch or peanut butter chips for chocolate chips, if desired. Makes about 2 pounds.

Nut Brittle

2 cups granulated sugar
1 pound butter (not margarine)
1 cup pecans or any nut you prefer

In large saucepan stir ingredients while cooking over medium heat til golden brown, 300 to 305 degrees F. Remove from stove and pour at once onto a metal jelly roll pan. Break into bite-size pieces when cool.

Peanut Butter Peanut Brittle

2 cups peanut butter
1 ½ cups light corn syrup
1 ½ cups sugar
¼ cup water
2 tablespoons butter
2 cups raw peanuts
1 teaspoon brown sugar, sifted
1 teaspoon vanilla extract
Butter

In double boiler warm peanut butter over low heat. Meanwhile, butter 2 large baking sheets and set aside. Butter sides of 3-quart saucepan.

In large saucepan combine sugar, corn syrup, and water. Cook and stir over medium heat til 275 degrees F on a candy thermometer (about 15 minutes).

Reduce heat to medium. Add 2 tablespoons butter and stir til melted. Add peanuts and cook and stir for 5 minutes or til candy starts turning brown and thermometer reaches 295 degrees F. Remove from heat.

Continue to stir. Add brown sugar and vanilla extract to candy. Gently stir til well-combined. Immediately pour into prepared cookie sheets. Work quickly and spread or stretch using 2 forks to lift and pull candy as it cools.

When cool break into pieces. Makes about 3 pounds.

SEA FOAM

3 cups sugar
½ cup white corn syrup
1 cup water
2 eggs whites, stiffly beaten.

In large saucepan combine ingredients and boil til mixture threads, at about 252 degrees F. Pour over beaten egg whites. Beat til mixture drops off spoon. Nuts may be added.

SOUTHERN PRALINES

1 cup sugar
1 cup packed brown sugar
½ cup light cream
¼ teaspoon salt
2 tablespoon butter
1 cup pecans

Line large baking sheet with aluminum foil. Butter aluminum foil. Combine sugars, cream, and salt in a large saucepan. Cook over medium heat, stirring constantly, to 228 degrees F.

Stir in butter and pecans. Cook to 236 degrees F. Cool 5 minutes.

Beat mixture with wooden spoon til slightly thick and candy just coats nuts, but doesn't lose its gloss.

Drop in large spoonfuls on buttered foil.

TURTLES

2 cups sugar
1 ½ cups corn syrup
3 cups cream
½ teaspoon salt
1 pound candy making chocolate

Prepare large baking sheet by buttering it well and dropping piles of 3 pecans each on tray. In saucepan combine sugar, corn syrup, 1 cup cream, and salt. Heat slowly to boiling, and stir til sugar is dissolved.

Cook to 234 degrees F. Add another cup of cream and heat again to 234 degrees F. Add third cup cream and heat to 238 degrees F or firm ball stage.

Place spoonful of caramel on top of nuts on baking sheet. Top with melted chocolate. Let cool. Makes approximately 82 pieces.

COOKIES

BOURBON BALLS

3 cups vanilla wafers, ground
3 tablespoons light corn syrup
1 ½ tablespoons cocoa, if desired
½ cup bourbon

In a large bowl combine ingredients. Combine 1 cup pecans and 1 cup powdered sugar. Roll dough into balls and roll balls in powdered sugar. Makes 35 balls.

BROWN SUGAR CRISPS

¾ cup packed brown sugar
¼ cup sugar
½ cup margarine, softened
1 egg
1 teaspoon vanilla extract
½ teaspoon allspice
½ teaspoon cinnamon
2 cups biscuit mix
½ cup chopped nuts

Preheat oven to 350 degrees F. In a large mixing bowl beat both sugars, margarine, egg, vanilla extract, allspice, and cinnamon til smooth and creamy. Stir in biscuit mix and nuts. Drop dough about 2 inches apart onto un-greased cookie sheets. Bake til light brown, 12 to 15 minutes. Immediately remove. Makes about 3 ½ dozen cookies.

BUTTERSCOTCH BROWNIES

¼ cup butter
1 cup packed brown sugar
1 egg beaten
1 teaspoon vanilla extract
½ cup flour
1 teaspoon baking powder
½ teaspoon salt
½ cup nut meats

Preheat oven to 350 degrees F. Melt butter and combine with remaining ingredients. Press into a 13 x 9-inch pan and bake for 30 to 35 minutes. Allow to cool and cut.

BUTTERSCOTCH PECAN SQUARES

14 ounces sweetened condensed milk
12 ounces butterscotch chips
2 ⅓ cups flour
½ teaspoon baking soda
½ teaspoon salt
10 tablespoons unsalted butter at room temperature
⅔ cup sugar
1 egg
1 teaspoon vanilla extract
½ cup chopped pecans

Preheat oven to 350 degrees F. Butter bottom and sides of a 13 x 9-inch pan. Line bottom and sides of pan with foil. In saucepan heat condensed milk and butterscotch chips over low heat and stir til chips melt.

In small bowl sift flour, baking soda, and salt. In large bowl beat butter and sugar til creamy. Beat in egg and vanilla extract til light and fluffy. Beat in flour mixture til dough just comes together. Reserve ½ to ⅔ cup of dough. Press the rest into bottom and ½-inch up the sides of pan. Pour butterscotch filling into dough. Crumble remaining dough on top. Sprinkle with pecans.

Bake til crust is golden brown, 30 to 35 minutes. Cool. Using foil, lift from pan and cut into squares or diamond shapes.

Championship Chocolate Chip Bars

1 ½ cups flour
½ cup packed light brown sugar
12 ounces chocolate chips, divided (2 cups)
14 ounces sweetened condensed milk
1 egg slightly beaten
1 teaspoon vanilla extract
1 cup chopped nuts
1 stick margarine, chilled

Preheat oven to 350 degrees F. In medium bowl combine brown sugar and flour. Cut in cold butter til crumbly. Stir in ½ cup chocolate chips and press into 13 x 9-inch pan. Bake 15 minutes.

Meanwhile in large bowl combine milk, egg, and vanilla extract. Stir in 1 ½ cups chocolate chips and 1 cup nuts.

Spread over baked crust. Bake 25 minutes or til golden brown, cool and cut unto bars.

Chocolate Chip Crisps

1 cup and 2 tablespoons flour
½ teaspoon baking soda
½ teaspoon salt
½ cup shortening
6 tablespoons sugar
6 tablespoons packed brown sugar
1 egg, unbeaten
Few drops hot water
2 cups cornflakes
6 ounces chocolate chips
½ teaspoon vanilla extract

Preheat oven to 375 degrees F. In small bowl sift flour, baking soda, and salt. In large bowl cream shortening, sugar, and egg til light and fluffy. Blend in flour mixture. Stir in hot water, vanilla extract, corn flakes, and chips. Drop by rounded teaspoon full onto cookie sheet and bake 10 to 12 minutes.

Chocolate Chip, Oatmeal, & Peanut Butter Cookies

1 ½ cups flour
1 teaspoon baking soda
1 teaspoon salt
1 cup shortening
¾ cup packed brown sugar
¾ cup sugar
2 eggs unbeaten
1 teaspoon hot water
1 cup chunky peanut butter
12 ounces chocolate chips
2 cups oatmeal
1 teaspoon vanilla extract

Preheat oven to 375 degrees F. In large bowl cream together shortening, brown sugar, sugar, peanut butter, and eggs. Dissolve baking soda in hot water and add. Mix in flour and salt. Add vanilla extract, chocolate chips, and oatmeal.

Drop by rounded tablespoons on cookie sheet. Bake for 8 minutes.

Coconut Thumbprints

½ cup butter flavored shortening
½ cup sugar
1 egg, separated
1 teaspoon vanilla extract
¼ cup flour
¼ cup salt
¼ teaspoon baking powder
⅔ cup coconut flakes
¼ cup thick jam or jelly preserves

Preheat oven to 375 degrees F. Grease baking sheet. At medium speed in large bowl cream butter, sugar, egg yolk, and vanilla extract. In small bowl sift flour, salt, and baking powder and add to creamed mixture. Blend well.

Form into 1-inch balls. Beat egg white til frothy. Dip balls into egg white and roll in coconut. Place on greased cookie sheets.

Make shallow depression in center of each cookie using thumb or base of a small spoon.

Place ½ teaspoon preserves in center of each. Bake for 8 to 9 minutes or til coconut begins to brown.

Cool on cookie sheets about 1 to 2 minutes and remove to cooling rack. Makes about 2 dozen cookies.

Cocoons

½ pound butter, softened
1 cup powdered sugar
2 cups flour
1 cup chopped nuts
1 tablespoon vanilla extract

In large bowl cream butter, add sugar and flour. Mix well and knead dough. Add nuts and vanilla extract. Knead again. Roll into oblong balls, about the size of the last joint of your little finger. They swell a lot.

Place on un-greased cookie sheet. Place in cold oven. "Light" oven and cook at 300 degrees F for 50 to 60 minutes or preheat oven to 300 degrees F and bake for 30 to 50 minutes, til golden brown on bottom. While still warm, roll in powdered sugar.

Congo Cookies

2 ¾ cups sifted flour
2 ½ teaspoons baking powder
½ teaspoon salt
⅔ cup shortening
2 ½ cups packed brown sugar
3 eggs
1 cup nuts
7 ounces chocolate chips
1 teaspoon vanilla extract

Preheat oven to 350 degrees F. In medium saucepan melt shortening over low heat and add brown sugar. Stir til well-mixed and allow mixture to cool slightly. Add eggs, 1 at a time, beating well after each addition. Add dry ingredients; nuts, chocolate chips, and vanilla extract.

Pour in greased 15 x 10-inch pan and bake for 35 minutes.

When almost cool, cut into finger-like bars and roll in powdered sugar.

CREAM CHEESE COOKIES

½ cup packed brown sugar
¼ cup margarine, softened
1 cup biscuit mix
½ cup chopped walnuts
8 ounces cream cheese, softened
¼ cup sugar
1 tablespoon lemon juice
2 teaspoons milk
½ teaspoon vanilla extract
1 egg

Preheat oven to 350 degrees F and grease 8 x 8-inch pan. In large bowl beat brown sugar and margarine til fluffy. Stir in biscuit mix and nuts til mixture is crumbly. Reserve 1 cup. Press remaining mix into pan. Bake for 12 minutes. In medium bowl mix cream cheese and sugar. Add lemon juice, milk, vanilla extract, and egg and beat til smooth. Spread mixture over crumb layer in pan. Sprinkle with reserved crumb mix. Bake til center is firm, about 25 minutes. Cut into 2-inch squares. Store in refrigerator.

DOUBLE CRUNCHERS

1 cup flour
½ teaspoon baking soda
¼ teaspoon salt
½ cup butter
½ cup sugar
½ cup brown sugar, packed
1 cup corn flakes, crushed
1 cup dry oats
½ cup coconut

Preheat oven to 350 degrees F. Sift together flour, baking soda, and salt and set aside. Beat butter, sugar, and brown sugar til light and creamy. Stir in egg and vanilla. Add this to flour mixture til well-combined. Stir in corn flakes, oats, and coconut.

Reserve ⅓ of the dough for tops and use the rest for the bottoms. To form cookies, roll batter into balls, smaller balls for tops, but even number of tops and bottoms. Flatten with floured bottom of a glass. Place on a greased cookie sheet. Bake bottom cookies for 8 to 10 minutes and 4 to 5 minutes for tops.

For the filling, melt over hot water: 6 ounce package chocolate chips, ½ cup powdered sugar, and 1 tablespoon water. Blend in a 3-ounce package soft cream cheese. Beat until smooth, cool and spread filling over larger cookies and top with small cookies.

FUDGIE PEANUT BUTTER BARS

1 package yellow cake mix
1 cup peanut butter
½ cup butter, melted
2 eggs

Filling

1 cup chocolate chips
1 ½ cups sweetened condensed milk
2 tablespoons butter
1 package coconut pecan frosting mix

In heavy saucepan combine chocolate pieces, sweetened condensed milk, and 2 tablespoons butter. Melt over low heat stirring constantly til smooth. Remove from heat and stir in frosting mix. In large bowl combine cake mix, peanut butter, ½ cup butter, and eggs. Preheat oven to 350 degrees F. By hand stir til dough holds together. Press ⅔ of dough into ungreased 13 x 9-inch pan. Reserve remaining dough for topping. Spread filling over dough in pan. Crumble reserved dough over filling. Bake for 20 to 25 minutes. Cool and cut into bars. Makes about 36 bars.

Lenora's Christmas Cookies

½ cup butter, softened
1 cup sugar
1 egg, beaten
1 teaspoon orange rind
1¾ cups flour
½ teaspoon salt
1 teaspoon baking powder

Preheat oven to 350 degrees F. In a large bowl cream together the butter and sugar. Add the egg and orange rind. Beat til smooth and creamy. Add flour, salt, and baking powder. Beat til smooth and creamy.

Roll dough to about ⅛-inch thick and cut with Christmas cookie cutters. Sprinkle with colored sugar. Bake for 10 minutes.

My personal favorite!

Merry Cheese Bars

1 cup flour
½ cup butter, softened
½ cup packed brown sugar
½ cup chopped nuts

Preheat oven to 350 degrees F. In large bowl combine flour, butter, and brown sugar.

Blend with mixer at low speed for 2 to 3 minutes til particles are fine. Stir in nuts. Reserve 1 cup of mixture for topping. Pat remainder in un-greased 8-inch square pan. Bake near center of oven for 8 to 10 minutes, or til lightly browned.

Filling

8 ounces cream cheese, softened
¼ cup sugar
2 tablespoons each of milk and lemon juice
¼ tablespoon vanilla extract

Prepare filling. Blend together cream cheese, sugar, milk, lemon juice, and vanilla extract to creamy.

Spread over partially baked crust. Sprinkle with reserved crumb mixture.

Return to oven for 20 to 30 minutes or til golden brown. Cool, cut into bars. Store in fridge, makes 24 to 30 bars.

Mexican Wedding Cakes

½ cup butter, softened
½ cup shortening
1 teaspoon vanilla extract
2 cups flour
1 cup chopped walnuts

Preheat oven to 400 degrees F. In large bowl combine ingredients in order given. Mix well before adding nuts.

Shape into small balls. Bake for 10 minutes. Roll in powdered sugar and store overnight before serving.

These cookies are very delicate.

Pineapple Cookies

⅓ cup shortening
⅔ cup sugar
2 eggs
½ cup nuts
⅔ cup well-drained crushed pineapple, save juice
1 ½ cup flour
3 teaspoons baking powder
Salt

Mix well and drop on cookie sheet. Bake in preheated 350 degree F oven about 15 minutes. For the topping mix powdered sugar into pineapple juice til stiff enough consistency to use as an icing for the cookies.

Peanut Butter Swirls

½ cup butter, softened
1 cup sugar
½ cup chunky peanut butter
1 egg
2 tablespoons milk
1¼ cups flour
¼ teaspoon salt
½ teaspoon baking soda
6-ounce package chocolate chips

In a large bowl combine everything except chocolate chips. Roll dough out on floured wax paper to approximately 15 x 8 x ¼-inch. Melt chocolate chips in a small saucepan over low heat and cool slightly. Spread on dough.

Roll up dough and place in refrigerator for 30 minutes to 1 hour. Preheat oven to 375 degrees F. Slice dough and bake for 8 to 10 minutes. Makes about 4 dozen.

Pecan Crispies

½ cup shortening
2 ½ cups packed brown sugar
½ teaspoon baking soda
2 eggs
2 ½ cups flour
½ cup butter, softened
½ teaspoon salt
1 teaspoon vanilla extract
1 cup chopped nuts

Preheat oven to 350 degrees F. Grease cookie sheet with butter. Sift flour, salt, and baking soda together. In a separate large bowl thoroughly cream shortening and sugar. Add eggs and vanilla extract. Add flour mixture. Add nuts and drop from teaspoon onto greased cookie sheet about 2 inches apart. Bake for 12 to 15 minutes. Makes about 6 dozen cookies.

Pecan Turtle Cookies

2 cups flour
1 cup packed brown sugar
½ cup butter, softened

Preheat oven to 350 degrees F. Mix the above ingredients in large bowl at medium speed for 2 to 3 minutes or til well-mixed and particles are fine. Pat firmly on jellyroll pan. Sprinkle 1 cup pecans over top.

Caramel Layer

1 cup butter
1 cup packed brown sugar
1 cup chocolate chips

In heavy saucepan combine butter and brown sugar. Cook over medium heat, stirring constantly, til entire surface of mix begins to boil. Boil 30 to 45 seconds.

Pour over crust and pecans. Bake 18 to 22 minutes or til entire surface is bubbly and light golden brown. Immediately pour chocolate chips over all, let melt slightly, and swirl for marbled effect. Cool completely and cut into bars. Makes 3 to 4 dozen bars.

Seven Layer Cookies

Preheat oven to 350 degrees F. Melt ¼ pound of butter and spread in a 13 x 9-inch pan. Then add, in layers, the following ingredients:

1 cup graham cracker crumbs
1 cup coconut
1 small package chocolate chips
1 small package butterscotch chips
1 can sweetened condensed milk
1 cup nuts

Bake for 30 minutes. Allow to cool and then cut into squares.

Sour Cream Cookies

2 cups sugar
1 cup shortening
2 eggs
1 teaspoon nutmeg

Preheat oven to 375 degrees F. In a large bowl mix the above ingredients together and then add:

1 cup sour cream
1 teaspoon baking soda
3 ½ cups flour

Drop from teaspoon onto baking sheets. Bake for 7 minutes.

Viennese Walnut Cookies

½ cup butter, softened
⅓ cup sugar
¼ teaspoon salt
1 teaspoon vanilla extract
1 ¼ cups flour
1 ⅓ cups finely chopped walnuts
Buttercream frosting

In large bowl cream butter, sugar, salt, and vanilla extract together. Blend in flour and nuts, using hands to form dough into a ball. Chill 30 minutes.

Preheat oven to 350 degrees F. Roll dough out on lightly floured board to a little less than ¼-inch thick. Cut with 2-inch cutter and place cookies on un-greased baking sheet.

Bake for 10 to 12 minutes. Cool on wire rack. Put pairs of cookies together with cream filling in middle. Top with swirl of frosting and a nut. Makes about 2 dozen.

Peace, Love, and Beauty ◊ A Living Memory

On the northeastern coast of the big island of Hawaii there once stood the village of Laupahoehoe. It was located on a point of land that protruded a little way into the ocean. It was a fairly ordinary seacoast village, but it commanded a beautiful view.

Immediately to the north were some large lava formations that caught incoming waves and sometimes sprayed foaming showers clear up onto the shore. To the south, the sea was uninterrupted until it came up against the tree covered cliffs that rose several hundred feet about the surf.

Then one day, many miles away, the earth trembled and stirred up the ocean's water in such a way that it could seemingly gather strength from its own movement. It built itself stronger and stronger as it spread outward, until it became a tidal wave, or tsunami. With no warning system available to them, the villagers were completely unaware of the danger. The tsunami produced three distinct waves which grew to between 30 and 50 feet high as they approached the shore.

The waves struck the little village with a sudden fury that allowed very few to escape as it completely destroyed the harbor area and the school. Only one teacher and two pupils from the school survived.

After it was finally over and the painful memories were dulled by time, it was realized that the beauty God had granted to Laupahoehoe Point still remained. Even the mighty tidal waves could not destroy that. Now the village has been rebuilt inland in a safer place and at Laupahoehoe Point there is a memorial park with picnic tables and where you can find peace if you look for it. This had become one of Dittie's and my favorite places in Hawaii.

Like this little village, Dittie too had a quiet beauty that surrounded her. It was found in her friends and family, in her many kindnesses, and in her very life. Although a tidal wave called Pneumonia may have destroyed Dittie as we knew her, the beauty granted to her by God still lives on. She too has been removed to a safer place, but when we search for her we can still find her peace, love, and beauty.

Recipes that are Special to You

The following pages are provided so you can document your own recipes that are special to you—your own "Recipes from the Heart," which can be passed on to your next generation.

MY SPECIAL RECIPES